THE
IDEAL BODY
FORMULA

THE
IDEAL BODY
FORMULA

How to Ditch Diet Culture and
*Achieve the **<u>NEW</u>** Ideal Body*

Tony Schober

TABLE OF CONTENTS

THE TURNING POINT

I Was Wrong

I thought I was a good coach. But it turned out I was wrong. My clients were happy, though. They got the weight loss results they hired me for. So I had no reason to believe I wasn't doing a good job. But my clients and I were both so caught up in Diet Culture that we didn't know any better.

The cycle always unfolded the same way. They'd hire me to lose weight. I'd create a custom meal plan for them to follow based on their food likes and dislikes, their body stats, and their activity levels. And I'd create a custom workout program for them to follow that was one part strength training and one part cardio. Then we'd work together to make sure they adhered to the plan, and I'd make adjustments along the way to ensure they kept dropping weight at 1-2 pounds per week.

You might be wondering what the problem is here. I certainly never thought there was a problem. I had a full client list. I had all kinds of testimonials and before-and-after pictures proving hiring me as a coach works. My clients left our 3 months together thrilled. And they'd keep coming back to me again and again whenever they needed to lose weight again.

And there was the problem. They kept coming back to me. On the surface, it might seem like I was the solution to their problem. They needed to lose weight, so they'd hire me, and I'd help them lose it. When we were done working together, they'd head off on their own and slowly start to gain the weight back. So later down the road, months or even years later, they'd send me an email asking to work together again.

What I didn't realize at the time was that I wasn't the solution to their problem – I was the person keeping their problem going. We only saw the weight loss. I never understood at the time that my coaching philosophy was actually keeping them stuck in a perpetual cycle of weight loss and weight gain, food and body obsession, and a diminished life experience – all while ensuring that their self-worth and confidence remained tied to the size of their body.

I was using weight loss as the sole determining factor of success. Well, that and my clients' happiness. But that happiness was simply tied to whether they lost weight or not.

It took a lot of time and a lot of soul searching before I admitted to myself that the approach I was taking, the same approach 99% of all fitness coaches take, was actually causing more harm than good. What we were all doing was keeping people stuck in Diet Culture and keeping people dependent on using their bodies to gain a sense of worth in society.

I started my company in September of 2011. At the time, the name of my company was Coach Calorie. Many of you reading this book have been with me from the very beginning, back when I was writing articles on weight loss. I was science-based, citing study after study showing what was best when it came to nutrition and exercise. And people loved my content. In a matter of a few months, my Facebook page went from 0 to over 100,000 followers. My articles were always at the top of Google search results. And I was making good money writing about what I loved.

THE IDEAL BODY FORMULA

So all signs were pointing to success. I had a working business and happy clients. Why would I ever think otherwise? It wasn't until years later when I realized I was experiencing the same weight loss and gain struggles as my clients were – the same struggles that most people stuck in the diet cycle experience.

I learned this the hard way after years of trying every dieting trick you can imagine. I got really big into meal timing. I'd make sure that most of my carb intake was eaten around my workouts so that they wouldn't be stored as fat. Because in my mind, if I ate carbs at night, I would never be able to lose weight. And then there was the phase when I thought I couldn't lose weight because I was putting a teaspoon of sugar in my oatmeal. Because sugar makes you fat, right?

The list of things I blamed for my weight loss struggles goes on and on. I was eating too much fruit. I needed to work out on an empty stomach so I could burn more fat. I wasn't eating enough protein. My thyroid hormone was too low. My testosterone was too low. I was eating too many grains. I was eating too many carbs. I wasn't eating enough carbs. I was eating carbs and fat in the same meal. There was too much fructose in my diet. I wasn't eating enough meals. I was eating too many meals.

What was interesting was most of these things all had science to back them up. But what I later realized is that none of the science or so-called proven studies really mattered if they couldn't be applied to my own life. This is when I understood that there was more to the story. What you do of course matters, but your own unique psychology is what determines the application of your desired behaviors. After all, most of us already know what to do and what's good for us. We just struggle understanding why we have trouble doing these things.

As I worked towards understanding why this was happening to me, I realized my entire approach to health and fitness was built on the wrong premise. This entire time I had been so focused on weight loss as the answer to all of my problems, when in reality, it was the focus on weight loss that was keeping me stuck in life.

What was I supposed to do? I felt stuck. My business was solely built around losing weight, calories, macros, fat loss exercise, and any other weight loss strategies that had science to back them up. I couldn't just stop pushing my philosophy. My family's financial security was dependent on keeping the status quo going.

But that all came to an end one random day. I kept getting question after question from followers about calories, carbs, sugar, weight loss, fat burning workouts, diets, fasts, meal timing, and all the other topics that have become normalized in Diet Culture. I had no problem with these questions before, but once you realize that Diet Culture is the source of all your problems, it's hard to surround yourself with that stuff anymore.

So that day I shut down my website, Coach Calorie. The same website that had made me hundreds of thousands of dollars, supported my family for years, and had over 20 million different people visit it. Overnight, gone. No explanation to anyone. Nothing.

I started a new website and rebranded my company Built Daily. I removed all those sleazy ads from my website that preyed on people's body insecurities. I changed my entire coaching approach, stopped creating meal plans, and stopped using all those Diet Culture tactics that previously lead to "success". I focused more and more on what truly transformed people for good.

Nowadays Built Daily is stronger than ever. My own life is in alignment. The food and body obsession is gone, and I'm at my own unique Ideal Body. My weight doesn't cycle over and over again, nor do my clients'. We have a strong community of like-minded people who want to ditch Diet Culture and achieve the

NEW Ideal Body. And in this book, I'm going to show you exactly how we're doing that.

Ditch Diet Culture

What exactly is Diet Culture anyways? I use a very simple definition. It's the never-ending pursuit to achieve society's universal beauty standard by any means necessary. And why would we do that? Because we've collectively decided to condition each other to believe that looking a certain way will make you more valuable in society. We've all decided that the way we are right now isn't good enough and that we should be striving to be one of the lucky few who can change their body and come out on top.

But that rarely happens. Instead, nearly everyone who is part of Diet Culture spends their entire life feeling less-than. They obsess over their food, body, and exercise constantly. They devote huge sums of money, time, and energy to changing their body so that they can feel more worthy as a human being. They track calories, fight through hunger, deprive themselves of enjoyable foods and experiences, do exercise they hate, and think about their bodies all the time. And for what? A chance to be one of the lucky 1% who succeed?

I can't think of anything else in life that so many people devote so much of their resources to for such an abysmal chance of success. We go on diet after diet hoping things will be different this time. By the way, a diet, in this sense, is simply eating to control your body. It doesn't need a fancy label to be considered a diet. It's any strategy that attempts to get you to eat less without directly addressing the root causes of the upward pressures on your eating. And studies show that 95% of these diets fail, yet we keep thinking we're going to be part of the 5% success rate. Personally, I think the chances are way less – like less than 1%.

Think about it. For a diet to work, it needs to go beyond just helping you lose weight. It has to be sustainable for life. If you make dietary and activity changes and you lose weight but are still struggling to this day, then it didn't work. In fact, what most people don't realize is that these Diet Culture tactics are the very things that cause the continued failure.

But let's also consider all the tomorrows and Mondays you've started over. Maybe it wasn't an official diet you were starting, but you were certainly trying to be better on those days after a night, weekend, or day of bad eating. In that case, I'd venture to say most people are starting over with their diets at least once a week if not every single day. But let's just say that it's only once per month you start over. Well... if you're currently still struggling with your body and it's been more than 10 years since you've tried to change it, then you've started over and failed 120 times. And you still haven't succeeded! If you had succeeded just once, that is still less than a 1% success rate. And the more likely scenario is people spend their entire adult lifetimes starting over. They end up on the perpetual dieting roller coaster – alternating periods of increased exercise and calorie budgeting with periods of less activity and less focused eating.

It's not structured diets that are failing us. Everyone knows that diets don't work. It's Diet Culture that is the culprit. Diet Culture is sneaky. It's really good at selling you a diet that doesn't make you think you're on one. Nowadays, weight loss attempts are repackaged and rebranded as lifestyle changes, or even getting healthy. This makes people feel like they are undertaking a noble cause. It gives them hope. Yet it still ends in failure. Why? Because noble cause or not, they still all use Diet Culture tactics. People still approach their health and fitness journey from the place of hating their bodies and feeling like they need to change them to feel more worthy in society.

It's this belief that your body is your worth that pushes you into behaviors that are out of alignment with your needs. Everything you do is for the purpose of looking a certain way. Better health, more confidence, improved happiness, and a better life experience all become dependent on what the scale or the mirror shows.

Diet Culture is not the solution to your problems. If it was, it would've worked by now. You have to stop confusing the possible with the probable. We will always know someone who succeeded with Diet Culture. When there are a quarter billion adults in the United States, and half those people tried to lose weight in the last year alone, you're bound to see some success – maybe even a lot in sheer numbers.

If 1,000,000 people have succeeded at a low carb diet, you're going to notice it. There will be pictures everywhere. There will be testimonials. There will be celebrities talking about them. You will have a friend that lost weight using one. But if 100 million adults have tried a low carb diet just once in their life, then that's still just a 1% success rate. And most people have tried one of these diets more than once. People are too willing to see a random person's success as proof something works, while completely ignoring their own 20 years of dieting history as proof it doesn't. Remember, the success rate of something that has never worked for you is 0%.

But it doesn't really matter, because all this is just referring to weight loss. True transformation is what we really want, and that is even more fleeting when you're participating in Diet Culture. Weight loss and transformation are not the same thing. Plenty of people lose weight but don't experience transformation. They just weigh less (temporarily, if it happens at all) but still experience insecurity, food obsession, and a constant focus on their body.

The answer to this problem is simple – ditch Diet Culture. When you decide to put that toxic culture behind you, that will be the moment in your life that things start to improve. That was the big inflection point in my life, and it's the same moment our community members experience too. That's when you get your first hints of real freedom and break free from the food and body prison you're currently in.

But you can't just ditch Diet Culture and assume everything is going to fall into place. That's just the start. The real work is just beginning. Over the years, Deanna, my wife and business partner, and I have worked with thousands of clients and have spoken to and heard the struggles of countless more. We took our own experiences overcoming Diet Culture and laid out a new process to follow. And this is the strategy we use to this day to help others get their life back. It's called the Ideal Body Formula.

The Ideal Body Formula™

Throughout our years of coaching and personal experiences, we were able to recognize a series of patterns among the people who truly succeeded in transforming themselves. And I don't mean just their bodies. Sometimes their bodies didn't change, but THEY changed. Independent of body change, people were improving their overall life experience. They were happier, healthier, more confident, and finally living life on their terms.

Sure, lots of people lost weight too. But that wasn't their primary goal. It's something that happened naturally when they focused on following the right process. It happened after they decided to ditch Diet Culture and all its surface level weight loss tactics promising big life changes that never materialized (and were never going to). Instead, they all succeeded once they turned inwards and worked through the real struggles that had been keeping them stuck and frustrated for a lifetime.

Here's what we realized: by focusing your attention away from weight loss and instead turning it towards healing your relationships with food, body, exercise, and mind, you could achieve your own unique Ideal Body. You shift your health and fitness journey away from a weight loss focus, and make it into one of healing. Because true change and transformation happen from the inside out. Your outside world becomes a function of the healing that's going on inside of you.

That's when we developed the Ideal Body Formula and started teaching it to others. The formula is simple. Your Ideal Body is the natural side effect of four core relationships – food, body, exercise, and mind. When those relationships are healed and in alignment, your Ideal Body is the natural side effect.

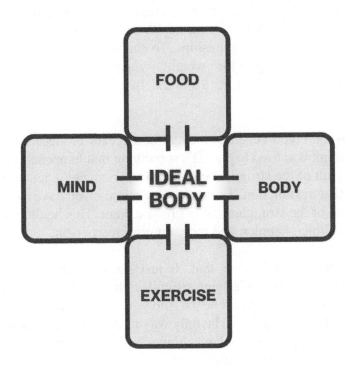

But make no mistake, the Ideal Body we're talking about here has nothing to do with society's Ideal Body. It has nothing to do with society's beauty standards. We're talking about the NEW Ideal Body. This body is about you.

Your Ideal Body isn't even a what – it's a when. It's the body you're in when you've healed your relationships with food, body, exercise, and mind. This is where you'll find your healthiest weight. Your unique Ideal Body might be smaller than your current body, or it might be the same or even bigger. That all depends on where you're starting from and the state of your four core relationships. But regardless of the similarities or differences to your current external appearance, you will be a better, healthier, more confident version of yourself, and will be living a more fulfilling life.

If you're struggling right now, it's because you have dysfunction in one or all of these four relationships. Your current life situation and the state of your health and fitness are simply the byproduct of those relationships. To change your life, you don't need to keep trying to lose weight – you just need to heal. Your healthiest weight will be a natural byproduct of that healing process.

The weight you've gained over these years or decades isn't something you tried to do – it's something that happened to you as a result of the struggles you were experiencing that stemmed from that dysfunction. To reverse that process you have to get to the root of the struggles and overcome them. This healing leads to a healthier, happier, and more empowered person.

Diet Culture doesn't do that. It just slaps a bandage on the wounds, aka your underlying struggles. In time, those bandages fall off. The wound never heals. And you get stuck in weight and diet cycles all your life. The only way to stop this cycle is to dig down and figure out what's going on in each of these four relationships and fix them.

Think about it. If you feel out of control with your eating, or if you're emotionally eating, or if you binge on the weekends, or if you mindlessly eat at night – how is following a diet or a calorie budget going to fix these things? It's not. It's going to arbitrarily restrict your food intake and force you to rely on willpower to override your dysfunctional relationship with food. And as anyone who has been stuck in the diet cycle can attest to – this never lasts.

But when you focus on healing your relationship with food and get down to the root causes of your eating struggles – your distrust around food, your struggle to meet your body's needs, and the disempowering association you have with food that is creating unnecessary restriction and deprivation – you eliminate these problems. You remove the upward pressures on your eating. Forced calorie restriction isn't necessary anymore. Your food intake naturally changes.

The same goes for your relationships with body, exercise, and mind. We have associations with our body that influence the way we see ourselves. And this impacts the way you eat and exercise. Diet Culture strategies can't heal your relationship with your body. In fact, they make it worse. They make everything worse.

The only way out of this vicious cycle of food obsession and body hate is to ditch Diet Culture and plug yourself into the Ideal Body Formula. You have to unsubscribe from society's conditioning that your body is your worth. You have to let go of all the shiny little diets, fat loss workouts, tips, tricks, tactics, and strategies that give everyone false hope. And then you have to start a new journey – one of personal discovery, development, and empowerment. One of healing.

The NEW Ideal Body – YOUR unique Ideal Body is the natural side effect.

How To Use This Book

This book exists for three reasons. The first is to get people to stop being victims of Diet Culture and all its disempowering beliefs. The second reason is to help you build confidence and belief that there is a new way and hope for getting you out from a lifetime of food and body struggles – that you can and will achieve your healthiest weight and full life experience if you follow the concepts I talk about. And finally, so that you'll consider joining our community so you can be supported and personally coached through the process of healing your relationships with food, body, exercise, and mind, so that you can achieve your Ideal Body.

This book is broken down into four main parts, each focused on one of the four relationships – food, body, exercise, and mind. Each relationship section is then further broken down into what we've found are key components to healing that particular relationship. These components are the most important parts of your journey. Most people understand they need to heal their relationships with food, body, exercise, and mind to finally succeed, yet they don't know how to do it. These components are what show you how.

You aren't going to find a bunch of little tips and tricks to implement with your eating and exercise in this book. If that's the kind of information you're looking for, you're going to be very disappointed. You're better off going to the diet section of your local bookstore and picking something from there. Diet Culture has plenty of that content for your consumption. There's no shortage of surface-level tactics getting people surface-level results.

But my guess is you're tired of that kind of stuff. It doesn't work. There's no one little trick that's going to change your life. Your problems are not the result of not knowing the exact calorie intake to eat. Your struggles aren't because you don't have the right magical macronutrient ratio. You haven't spent the last 10+ years struggling with your food and body because you haven't tried fasting, cleansing, cutting carbs, or some other gimmicky strategy.

Your struggles go deeper. And this book helps you go deeper. To some, it might even feel like a form of therapy. Its focus is on helping you change the way you think about your food, body, exercise, and mind. Because the meaning you have attached to those things right now is what is causing so much of your frustrations and failures. So if you want to get out of the downward spiral, you have to start looking at things differently. You need new perspectives, beliefs, and meaning attached to your health and fitness journey.

Some of the things in this book might be things you already know. Others will be huge epiphanies for you. Yet other parts will be worded in a way that you've never heard before, and that will complete the connection and finally help the concepts sink in.

It's also worth noting that this book isn't for people with extreme views. There are extreme views in both the Diet Culture and even the anti-Diet Culture communities. While the extremes in one community might push weight loss at all costs, the extremes in the other community might even shame you for having any desire to lose weight. Either way, you end up losing your body autonomy.

When I first broke free of Diet Culture, the vocal minorities in these groups made it feel like I didn't have a place to call home. So I created my own community of like-minded people. I see my views as more moderate in nature, but depending on where you are on the Diet Culture / anti-Diet Culture spectrum, they might even seem extreme to you. But there is something to learn from both communities, and I've done my best to find the common ground and add to it.

Go into this book with an open mind. You will quite possibly have a lot of objections to the things I say. There will be a lot of "yeah buts". This is normal. It happens anytime someone is challenging your beliefs. But understand if you hold onto your limiting beliefs of the past, you will continue to get the same outcomes in your future. Only by healing your relationships with food, body, exercise, and mind will you be able to break free of the food and body prison you're in. And to do that will require an open mind and an adoption of new more empowering beliefs.

All that said, I consider myself a very down to earth person. So most of what I write is grounded in common sense and proven application in our coaching practice. If it made it into this book, it's because it has been tested countless times on both Deanna and me, as well as the thousands of people who are part of our community and programs. Point being – these things work. They heal you. And they transform you. So you can be confident that I'm not just speaking in theoretical or ideological tones. I'm in the trenches putting these concepts to work with proven success.

While there is plenty of behavioral advice in this book, you're also going to notice that I approach health and fitness with the understanding that your behaviors naturally change as your relationships with food, body, exercise, and mind change. That's because as you heal, you see your journey through a different lens. Your beliefs and perspectives around food and body change. YOU change. You transform into a different identity. And that identity naturally brings with it new behaviors and outcomes. That's what happens when you go deep and heal.

As a coach, my goal is not just to get you results while you work with me. It's not even my goal to have you maintain your results. I want you to continue growing and transforming – for life. If I'm the same person 10 years from now, I'd consider that a failure. I want my clients to develop a growth mindset – not a maintenance existence. I want to empower them to see their full potential.

I can't do this focusing on body change and weight loss. I can only do this through transformation. Transformation is about changing who you are – not what you look like. Again, your physical appearance will very likely change as a result of changing who you are and how you interact with food, your body, exercise, and your mind. But that's just one of the many potential side effects you'll experience in your life as a result of healing and transformation.

So get out a highlighter and mark any parts that really resonate with you. Read through the entire book from start to finish. Then go back to any sections you feel like you need the most work with. Make this journey your own. Heal the parts that need the healing. Continue nurturing the parts that don't. Your Ideal Body will be the natural side effect.

PART I:

RELATIONSHIP WITH FOOD

CHAPTER 1

NAVIGATING HUNGER

Stop Counting Calories

Like most people, I thought that I had to count calories to achieve my goals. Weight loss and calorie counting went together like peanut butter and jelly.

The practice of setting a calorie budget and then tracking everything you eat is so ingrained in Diet Culture that most people never even stop to question whether it's the right approach to take.

As someone who loves numbers, data, and tracking things, calorie counting was right up my alley. The mere suggestion from someone saying I shouldn't do it was met with laughter, arrogance, annoyance, and defensiveness.

After all, I had all the proof I needed that it worked. When I tracked calories, I lost weight. And when I wasn't tracking calories, I wasn't making any progress.

I knew myself better than everyone else. At least I thought I did.

But calorie counting had one big negative side effect that I couldn't see for the longest time – it kept me stuck using food as a tool for controlling my body instead of using it as a way to feel my best. When you use food to control your external appearance instead of to mentally, emotionally, and physically feel your best, you get caught up in a lifetime of food obsession, diet culture, weight cycling, and body image struggles.

It got to the point where it felt like I was eating calories instead of food.

Turns out, calorie budgeting – aka the process of setting a calorie goal and then trying to hold that line at all costs – was the very thing keeping me stuck and frustrated.

It kept me focused on the wrong things. Instead of getting down to the root of my food issues and healing them, I remained focused on trying to lose weight using math.

If I eat 2000 calories and burn 2500, I'll lose weight. So all I need to do is set a calorie budget for 2000 calories, right? It doesn't work that way. Sure, if you eat less than you burn, you will lose weight. No one is arguing that. The issue is and always has been being able to maintain that energy deficit.

People think just setting a calorie budget and deciding to eat a certain amount of food is what results in you eating that amount of food. It's not.

How much you eat isn't a byproduct of the calories you say you're going to eat; it's a side effect of your relationship with food. And the more you try to control your food and calories, the more they end up controlling you.

Setting an arbitrary calorie budget does work if you define "work" as ignoring your underlying food struggles, losing a little weight for a short while, and then gaining it all back.

If that is what you consider working, then you were just like me and most other people who defend calorie counting. But if you're going to attribute calorie budgeting to the cause of your weight loss, then you also need to attribute it to the cause of your resulting weight gain and continued participation in Diet Culture.

Why? Because slashing calories in the face of an unhealthy relationship with food attempts to just put a bandaid over your underlying struggles. These struggles don't go away simply because you say you're going to eat less. Setting a calorie budget and then doubling down on willpower just pushes those struggles beneath the surface for a little while.

But they are still there, creating upward pressures on your eating. Until one day those struggles resurface, and no amount of saying you're going to eat xxxx amount of calories will be able to overpower the consequences of ignoring your body's needs.

Most of us have been through that process many times. And each time you go through that cycle, you reinforce the idea that calorie counting works, while at the same time keeping yourself stuck in Diet Culture's grips.

So does calorie budgeting work? It can – assuming you already have a healthy relationship with food. But if that was you, you probably wouldn't be reading this book.

For someone who struggles with their relationship with food, calorie budgeting is a crutch that gives you a false sense of success. If you want to heal, you're going to have to put it aside for now. Because your struggles are much deeper than what MyFitnessPal can solve.

How Many Calories Should I Eat?

This is easily the number one question people asked me 10 years ago when I was a weight loss coach, who himself, was stuck in Diet Culture.

THE IDEAL BODY FORMULA

THE IDEAL BODY FORMULA

We've all asked that question. We try out several different calorie calculators, search the internet for equations, and ask people for advice on how much we should eat to lose weight.

Interestingly, you've most likely already consumed calories at a level that would result in weight loss if you had been able to stick it out.

But we think there's some magic number of calories to eat. As if a 100-200 calorie difference is some kind of success breaker. It's not, by the way.

The issue has never been you not knowing how many calories to eat. All that information is readily available to you. And even if you're still unsure, simply cutting a few hundred calories each week until you see weight loss would eventually get you to an intake that "works".

Point being – asking how many calories you should eat is the wrong question to be asking. It's rooted in Diet Culture and body control and doesn't address the real question you should be asking...

Why am I not already eating at a calorie intake that would result in me feeling my best?

Asking about calorie intakes keeps you focused on outcomes and side effects. Remember, how much you eat isn't dictated by a calorie budget – it's determined by your relationship with food.

The second question addresses that relationship. It gets you down to the source of your eating struggles and the cause of your overeating.

You can go use a calorie calculator and try to set a calorie budget all you want, but saying you're going to eat 1200 calories, even though that will result in weight loss for the majority of people, is not going to work if you haven't healed your relationship with food.

Eating 1200 calories doesn't fix your emotional eating struggle. It doesn't fix your binge eating. It doesn't fix your out of control nighttime or weekend overeating. It doesn't fix your distrust around fun foods. And it doesn't get you more in touch with your hunger cues.

In the long term we don't decide how much we eat. How much we eat is a side effect of our relationship with food, body, exercise, and mind. You might be able to set a calorie budget and follow it in the short term, but unless you address your underlying food and body struggles, there will always be long-term upward pressures on how much you eat. And no amount of artificially restricting calories is going to fix these things. In fact, it makes all of these issues worse. Remember – your body doesn't care about your physique goals. Its job is to get you to meet its needs.

There will come a time when calorie counting can be a useful tool in achieving specific goals. But until you heal your relationship with food, taking a calorie centric approach is a liability to your success.

The Biggest Influence On Your Eating

How much you eat is determined by the meaning you've attached to food.

It's not determined by an arbitrary calorie budget – at least not in the long term. You will always revert to a level of eating that corresponds to the meaning you've attached to food.

I was thinking about this when my then 7yo son got an ice cream sandwich out of the freezer. He stood there at the trash can unwrapping it, throwing all the little torn pieces of paper wrapping into the trash.

Then, once it was fully unwrapped, he threw the whole damn ice cream sandwich into the trash too.

This triggered me horribly. And when I asked him why he threw it away, he simply said he didn't want it.

That experience really got me thinking about food and why two people can have two different experiences witnessing the same situation, and how it influences our eating as a whole.

When we're born, we have a very basic view of food. It is sustenance. It is energy. We eat when we're hungry and stop when we're satiated.

It's a very simple process that happens on an unconscious level.

But over the years we start attaching new meaning to food based on experiences we have and beliefs passed down to us from parents, society, diet culture, etc.

When my son threw that ice cream sandwich in the trash, it felt like a waste of money. I had attached meaning to food that went beyond simple sustenance.

Over time, I've also attached other meanings to food – relief, satisfaction, entertainment, pain, guilt, fear, and health… to name a few.

These dynamics are what create my relationship with food and determine what, how much, when, and why I eat.

This is why we focus so much on improving our relationship with food in our Built Daily Mentorship program. By changing the meaning you've attached to food, you influence your eating for the better – permanently.

That doesn't mean you can't attach meaning to food that's beyond basic sustenance. Not all nurtured dynamics are bad. Some can add to your life experience.

But good or bad, the meaning you've attached to food is still the biggest determinant of how much you eat. So understanding your dynamic with it is necessary for any true change to occur.

Hunger Is An Asset

Most people have a dysfunctional relationship with hunger. They see it as something that needs to be suppressed, avoided, and fought.

But why?

We don't think twice about honoring our body's other signals...

You're thirsty? You drink.

You're tired? You sleep.

You think something is funny? You laugh.

You hurt yourself? You tend to the pain.

You're bored? You do something.

But when you're hungry? GO AWAY, WHY ARE YOU HERE!

If you really think about it, it's not so much about the hunger. Instead, it's all about your relationship with food and what it represents to you.

For a lot of people, food has a strong association with body image struggles. In other words, they see food as the reason they don't like the way they look.

THE IDEAL BODY FORMULA

Clothes don't fit? It's because of FOOD!

Afraid to wear a swimsuit? It's because of FOOD!

People criticizing your body? It's because of FOOD!

Avoid seeing people? It's because of FOOD!

Feeling less valuable as a human? It's because of FOOD!

No wonder we treat hunger differently. It's a constant reminder that we don't like the way we look and that we feel less-than.

But if you're hungry, it's for a reason. Your body is asking for an unmet need – usually calories (aka energy). Just like how thirst tells you that you need fluids, hunger is telling you that you need food and nutrients.

It's an asset, not a liability. It's meant to be honored – not feared. The problem arises when we tie our self-worth to our body. When that happens, food becomes a tool for body control, which is really just another way of saying you use food to control your self-worth.

So anything that threatens your self-worth is subconsciously labeled a liability. Food and calories are now the enemy, and anything that drives you to eat becomes a threat.

That's why we employ all kinds of appetite-suppressing strategies in an effort to fight hunger. We drink caffeine, take pills, undergo surgery, set food rules such as no eating after 6 pm, or just flat out ignore our hunger.

Ironically, the most effective way to suppress your hunger is to honor it and eat. Hunger is a sign your body needs energy – not food suppressing tactics. Artificially suppressing your appetite doesn't make the need for energy (food) go away.

For a lot of people, they've ignored their hunger for so long they don't even know what it truly feels like to honor it. They've delegated their hunger to external cues like calorie counting, which has served to only divorce them from their own body's intuition.

One of the first things you experience when you let go of calorie counting is a turning inwards and reconnecting with your body's hunger cues. These hunger cues are huge assets in your health and fitness journey. Once you're in tune with them, they become a highly accurate calorie regulator – far more effective than any arbitrary calorie budget a calculator would have you eat.

Eating When You're Hungry

When you've relied on calorie counting all your life to determine how much to eat, it can be scary learning how to eat based on your hunger cues.

There are a lot of fears and unknowns. And when you combine that with an unhealthy relationship with food, you can feel a little like a fish out of water.

When do I eat? How much do I eat? What do I eat?

Remember, calorie budgeting only provided you with a false sense of comfort. It made you feel like you were eating an optimum amount of food. But in reality, only your body can tell you what is optimal.

The process for navigating hunger once you do away with the calorie counting crutch is so simple that you're probably going to dismiss it right away. But hang in there, because it all gets easier as you move through the process of healing.

So how do you do it? You eat when you're hungry but not starving, and you stop when you're satisfied but not stuffed.

That's it. It's simple because it's supposed to be simple. Eating isn't supposed to be complicated. You're not supposed to need a PhD in nutrition to eat, nor a hundred food rules or diets to follow in order to live optimally.

But despite the simplicity of this process, most people will find it very difficult for a couple of reasons.

First, counting calories feels objective. You're either eating a certain amount of food or you're not. There's little room for flexibility, which ironically, is part of the problem. On the other hand, analyzing hunger feels very subjective. There's quite a bit of uncertainty involved.

But that's only at the beginning, and only because you're currently divorced from your body's hunger cues. As you get in the reps of checking in with your hunger, using tools such as the hunger scale, your hunger becomes less and less subjective and abstract, and more and more objective and measurable.

The second reason people find it difficult to honor their hunger has less to do with breaking up with calorie calculators, and more to do with your body image.

We already know why calorie counting doesn't work when you have an unhealthy relationship with food. Your underlying struggles don't get solved. They just get bandaged over in the short-term, and that creates upward pressures and inconsistencies with your eating.

But that doesn't explain why people then struggle with the simple advice of eating when you're hungry but not starving, and stopping when you're satisfied but not stuffed.

Your eating doesn't happen in a vacuum. Remember, your Ideal Body is the side effect of 4 relationships – food, body, exercise, and mind.

These relationships have an interdependent relationship with each other. They function alone and need to be healed individually, but they also affect each other and create a synergistic effect.

This is important to understand because so much of our eating is influenced by our body image and how we perceive ourselves.

A negative body image forces us into eating decisions that aren't in our best interest. When you don't like the way you look or you hate your body, it's really hard to listen to your body's cues.

Instead, you distrust your body. You rely on calorie trackers and other external tools like the scale. And you base your eating decisions, knowingly or not, around whether they will help you like your body.

You end up honoring your weight loss instead of your hunger. You ignore your body's needs and tell yourself "no" when you're hungry.

The association made is that food and calories equal hating your body. Food is a liability. Your body is a liability.

That's why people struggle with navigating their hunger when they drop calorie counting. First, they've smothered their hunger for a lifetime and have a hard time hearing their hunger cues. And second, they aren't really navigating their hunger at all – they're navigating their self-worth through food.

We will soon get to the section of the Formula that focuses on healing your relationship with your body, but for now, understand that it's normal to be scared, upset, angry, frustrated, or any other emotion over the idea of giving up calorie counting.

This is part of the healing process. But if you stick with it you will learn to trust yourself again. And when the time comes when you've completely healed your four relationships and could theoretically reintroduce calorie counting in a healthy way, I think you might find that you don't want to. You don't need it. And you feel freer and more in touch with your body without it.

The Daily Reset

It was 8 pm and I was starving. I wanted to eat but felt like I couldn't.

I was having an internal struggle – do I go over my calories for the day and kill off the hunger pangs, or do I suck it up until I fall asleep for the sake of weight loss?

This used to happen a lot, and I would mistakenly try to tough it out. I might've made it through the night, but eventually, the hunger would catch up to me, and I'd end up overeating or bingeing anyway.

The turning point for me was asking myself a very important question when the hunger pangs set in – "If I weren't trying to lose weight, would I eat right now?"

The answer was always yes, which meant ignoring my hunger was prioritizing my weight loss over my body's needs.

And make no mistake, whether you try to prioritize weight loss over your hunger or not – your body will always prioritize its needs. And those needs scream louder and louder the more they get ignored. Suppressing this hunger until you go to bed doesn't make the need go away.

Our meals don't exist in isolation. And our bodies don't work on a 24-hour clock. Just because you make it through a day of hunger suffering, it doesn't mean you get a fresh slate to work with the next day.

Meals and calories have an accumulative effect. Each successive meal has an effect on the next.

What and how you eat today affects how you think, feel, and act tomorrow.

There's a big misconception out there that every day is a new day – that you get to start with a clean slate, and whatever or however you ate yesterday has no impact on the following day.

From a mindset perspective, this is and should be true. In other words, if you totally mess up your eating today, you should learn from the experience and then put the thoughts and feelings of the situation behind you and move on. Holding onto the guilt, shame, and negative self-talk serves no purpose.

However, when it comes to the accumulating effects of your eating, you don't get to start over tomorrow. The last meal you just ate will affect the next one you eat. The next will affect the next. Today's eating will affect tomorrow's eating, and how you eat this week will affect what happens the week after that.

There are cause and effect forces always at play. Strong-arming your way through today on low calories, with the idea that if you could just make it through the day and get to sleep that it will have been a success, is misguided thinking. You don't get a clean slate tomorrow.

Fight and ignore your hunger today, and tomorrow you're starting at a disadvantage. Hormone changes and remnant feelings of restriction and deprivation are just under the surface, and they will add risk to your eating.

Going to sleep has nothing to do with your eating (outside of lack of sleep influencing the types or quantities of foods you eat). Your eating is one continuous cycle. Sleep just happens to occur every night. It isn't an eraser.

So the answer is very simple. If you're hungry – eat. It doesn't matter what time it is. It doesn't matter how long it's been since your last meal. It doesn't matter if you seem hungrier today compared to yesterday. You always honor your hunger over your weight loss. Because if you don't consciously make that decision in the moment, your body will eventually make that decision for you anyway, but at a higher cost.

You're hungry for a reason. You might not totally understand why yet, but your body knows it needs something with 100% confidence. While you continue to work on understanding and healing your relationship with food, honor that hunger – always. Start learning to trust again that your body knows best.

CHAPTER 2

PERMISSION-BASED EATING

Eat What You Want

Part of healing your relationship with food means giving yourself unconditional permission to eat whatever you want, whenever you want it, in as much quantity as you want.

When I tell people that, they're usually in disbelief. They immediately think that if they did that, all they'd do is eat pizza, cookies, cake, and ice cream all day, every day. They'd gain weight, get fat, and feel miserable about themselves.

The resistance to accepting this statement comes from focusing on the "whatever," "whenever," and the quantity of what they eat, instead of focusing on the "want" part. They're confusing permission with desire. They're assuming their "cans" and their "wants" are the same and always will be.

It's normal to think that. But you have to remember one very important thing – what you want to eat as an active participant in Diet Culture is not the same thing you'll want once you free yourself from the food prison you're in. Your wants will change as you do.

THE IDEAL BODY FORMULA

Before I made my first foray into permission-based eating, I was the kind of person who planned out their entire week's worth of meals beforehand, each meal picked so that its calorie content would fit into the calorie budget I set for the day.

My planned diet was all whole foods, of course. Because eating junk food was bad and wouldn't allow me to lose weight.

But much to my dismay, I was never able to stick to my perfect diet. Maybe I could for a day or two or possibly even for the entire workweek. But when nighttime came, or the weekend arrived, things would start to fall apart.

At the time, I was not giving myself permission to eat whatever I wanted. I was following a set of food rules, "can'ts," and "shouldn'ts." Because it's what I thought I had to do to succeed.

Like most people, the lack of permission around food was leading to the very outcome I didn't want. I felt restricted and deprived, and I'd just end up eating the foods anyways.

And when I did end up eating those foods, it wasn't from a place of permission and abundance. It came from a place of scarcity and a biological drive to just give in. Food was the one running the show.

I was fed up with the cycle and needed to do something different. So I flipped the script and decided I was going to give myself unconditional permission to eat whatever I wanted, whenever I wanted it, and in whatever quantities I wanted.

I went to the grocery store to do my shopping for the week. But I didn't have anything planned. No meal plan. No shopping list. I was going to walk up and down the aisles to buy whatever I wanted.

And that's exactly what I did. I bought cereal for breakfast. Fried chicken tenders for lunch. Frozen pizzas for dinner. Hostess

Cupcakes for snacks. And I even bought soda to drink. I rarely drink soda, but I wanted it, so I got it.

As I went up and down the aisles choosing my food this way, I felt an overwhelming sense of freedom wash over me. A lifetime of food rules to which I had been imprisoned was shattered.

It was a very emotional shopping experience for me, one I'll never forget. Because it was in that moment that I realized just how hard I had been on myself all these years in the quest to lose weight.

When I got home, I started my new "diet" immediately. That first day, I ate everything I had bought and wanted to eat. And I did it with full permission and no guilt or shame attached.

It was great. But it didn't last long. By the next day at lunchtime, I realized that I really didn't want the lunch I picked out anymore. I had gotten the desire to eat junk food out of my system, and I actually wanted something a little more nutritious.

I went back to the store and got some different food that would make me feel better. It was what I wanted to eat – not what I thought I should eat or had to eat.

By the end of the week, my diet was mostly whole foods again. But this time, I was eating from a place of freedom. There was no one telling me what I had to eat. No food rules. I was running the show.

And that's what permission-based eating will do for you too. The timetable might not be the same, but the process will be similar.

Permission is the process of taking back control from food. It forms the foundation of your eating decisions and allows you to feel empowered around food.

I started eating what I wanted, whenever I wanted, in whatever quantities I wanted. But those wants were no longer pizza, ice cream, cupcakes, and soda. My wants shifted to what made me feel my best. Leaving behind Diet Culture allowed me to change, and my wants changed as I did.

Creating Healthy Boundaries Around Food

Permission-based eating isn't the same thing as a free-for-all. Nor is permission a synonym for "yes" or "eat it". It's not a behavior – it's an underlying mindset, an attitude towards food, that helps you make the best choices for yourself both in the short term and the long term. It's what gives you the space to make eating choices from a place of "I do/don't want" instead of "I can't/shouldn't have."

Giving yourself permission starts NOW. You don't wait until you're presented with a food choice before giving yourself permission to eat it. You don't say "I'm GOING TO give myself permission". You give it. Now. Because a lack of a permissive state right now is what drives the compulsions later.

Giving yourself permission now creates a healthy and empowering atmosphere surrounding your eating. This leads to one of the biggest benefits of permission-based eating – the establishment of healthy boundaries around food.

A healthy boundary around food is not the same thing as a food rule. Diet Culture preaches food rules. These rules are very black and white, pass/fail, and are pushed onto you by people, programs, books, etc., that know nothing about you, your physiology, your psychology, your goals, or your unique situation. A healthy boundary is chosen by you, while a food rule is chosen for you.

A food rule is like trying to fit a square peg into a round hole. It attempts to force you to adapt to a diet, as opposed to letting your diet adapt to you. And worst of all, food rules don't solve any of your problems – they just try to bandage over them by taking a very mechanical outside-in approach to your eating.

If you're struggling with overeating at night, a food rule that might be imposed would be "no eating after 6pm". On the surface, it seems like that should work. After all, you're overeating at night, so if you don't eat at night, the problem is solved. Right? Wrong.

It's not problem solved. It's symptom treated. And that's what food rules do – they treat your symptoms. They slap a temporary bandaid on your underlying struggles, which might make you believe they work, until they don't. And then you think your solution is more black and white thinking, more willpower, more abstaining, more lines in the sand – more food rules that never worked in the first place.

Eating constraints imposed upon you from external forces will always create a disempowering feeling around food born out of an "I can't have" attitude. Food rules always keep the food in power and leave you feeling helpless around it.

The alternative to food rules is healthy boundaries around food. Healthy boundaries are born out of a place of "I don't want" – an empowering feeling rooted in personal autonomy and body respect. You are the one who decides whether to eat something or not, not because you can't control yourself around food, but because behaving in a certain way doesn't make you feel your best.

Boundaries are necessary for any healthy relationship to thrive, and your relationship with food is no different. We construct these boundaries to protect ourselves. They are in place so we can feel our best mentally, emotionally, and physically.

From the outside looking in, a healthy boundary around food and a food rule can LOOK exactly the same to an observer, but they feel very different to the person carrying out the behavior.

The difference between eating the same food and having two different outcomes is your mindset. That mindset determines how you feel when you eat. Without the mindset, you're not truly practicing permission-based eating – you're just eating and praying you'll be able to stop.

It's a nuance, but it's a big-impact nuance. Because how you feel when you eat right now determines how you will eat in the future. A healthy boundary can be implemented for life, as it aligns with your identity and helps you feel empowered. It leads to improved consistency over time.

Food rules don't align with you (remember the square peg and round hole analogy). They don't come from a place of permission. Nor do they last, as they don't address the underlying struggle that leads to the unwanted behavior you're trying to bandage over.

For example, I choose not to eat fried food. Not because I can't have it or because there's a food rule in place rooted in body control. Instead, I choose not to eat fried food because I don't want it. It's a healthy boundary rooted in self-care and body respect. When I eat it, I feel horrible, so I'll only consume it on the rarest of occasions. I don't miss it. I don't feel deprived of it. I don't feel like the food is calling out to me.

And unconditional permission was the mindset that led me to that healthy boundary. Giving myself permission to eat it provided the space to understand it wasn't something I truly wanted for myself. I could have it if I wanted, but I chose not to.

Scarcity vs Abundance

If you could only choose one meal to eat for the rest of your life, would it be M&Ms or a salad? Starting tomorrow, you have to eat it every time you're hungry—for breakfast, lunch, dinner, and everything in between—forever.

I asked this question to my social media community, and the answer was very interesting. The majority of people said they would eat the M&Ms. I then asked them if they felt they had a healthy relationship with food. The majority of people said they didn't.

This wasn't all that surprising to me. When you have an unhealthy relationship with food, one of the things you tend to do is put food up on a pedestal. You attach disempowering meaning to many foods and label them as off-limits.

This does two things. First, it makes the food feel scarce. Like most things in life, scarcity adds value. It doesn't matter if it's artificial scarcity or real scarcity; if it feels like it's in short supply, it becomes more valuable in the eyes of the beholder.

Anyone who lived through the early days of the COVID pandemic remembers how scarce toilet paper became. The scarcity changed people's behaviors and made them act irrationally.

The same thing happens with perceived gas shortages. When word gets around that gas is in short supply, people are quick to fill up their tanks, whether they need gas or not. Scarcity creates fear, which leads to people overvaluing things in the moment. This leads to more irrational decisions that aren't always in your best interest or the interest of the community as a whole.

Food is very similar. The only difference is the scarcity we feel is self-created. By labeling foods as good or bad, following arbitrary food rules, fearing food's impact on our weight, and eating from a place of no permission, we create scarcity and drive up the value of the very foods we feel like we shouldn't eat.

Which leads me to the second thing: placing the foods you want off-limits makes you eat them. Ironic, isn't it?

Scarcity creates demand. The less of something you feel there is, the more you want and value it. When you eat too few calories and food becomes scarce, there's an increase in food-seeking behaviors. This over-restriction in food intake results in you eating more food than you would have if you had just eaten from a place of abundance and fueled your body properly.

When you place fun foods off limits, they immediately become scarce. Banning them creates more intensity and allure around them, and you just want them more. Eventually, you do eat them, and usually in greater quantities.

When you eat from a place of scarcity, it drives what you call the last-supper mentality. You're always in a state of feeling like you can't have a particular food. So when you do inevitably eat it, you end up eating it in larger quantities than is desirable because you know that starting tomorrow, you won't be able to have it again. So you get your fill now.

This is the reason so many people feel out of control around particular foods. They blame addiction to sugar or label certain foods as triggering. And while food does have some physiological effects on your body that might drive your desire to eat, the bigger driver is your self-imposed psychology and the food prison you continue to keep yourself locked in.

When you let yourself out of that prison, neutralize scarcity with abundance, and give yourself permission to eat what you want, food loses its intensity. Off-limit foods lose their value and allure, and the food-seeking behaviors you try to suppress diminish.

THE IDEAL BODY FORMULA

M&Ms are no longer this amazing chocolatey goodness that is so bad yet oh so good. They're just food—food that either meets your needs or doesn't. Food that either makes you feel your best or doesn't.

So as you heal your relationship with food, you start eating food again instead of labels and feelings. You're able to recognize what's best for you and gravitate towards the foods that meet your needs and make you feel your best.

Because that's really what scarcity and abundance are all about. Most people think of scarcity as something that's really rare, and abundance as something that's overflowing beyond capacity.

But I like to think of it more simply. Scarcity means not having or being enough, and abundance means having or being enough. Scarcity means your needs aren't being met, while abundance means they are.

Feeling abundant around food means you're eating enough calories to feel and perform your best and enough of the types of foods that will satisfy you.

10 years ago, I wouldn't have had to think twice about whether I'd want M&Ms or a salad for the rest of my life. It was M&Ms all day, every day. But now? M&Ms are great, but only in small doses. Eat more than that, and I'll hear my body screaming for nutrition. So these days, I'm taking the salad, and it's not even close.

Your goal is to create an atmosphere where you take fun foods for granted. Because when you do, you don't eat as many of them. As soon as fun foods seem scarce, as soon as you feel like they're going to be taken away from you, that's when you want them most, and that's when you tend to overindulge in them.

Permission, healing, and abundance got me out of the intense food moments of the now that were driven by the disempowering psychology of my past, and allowed me to honor what I truly wanted and needed in order to feel my best, not just right now, but for the rest of my life.

The Binge / Restrict Cycle

Restricting calories and depriving yourself of satisfaction in your diet has a very predictable cause and effect. These behaviors tend to lead to the exact opposite of what you want to happen. And that leads to more restriction and deprivation. The cycle repeats and repeats. This is called the binge/restrict cycle.

While you might not experience a full out binge, the cycle is still the same. Call it the overeat/restrict cycle if you want. Regardless, it's a self-reinforcing downward spiral that you need to get yourself out of.

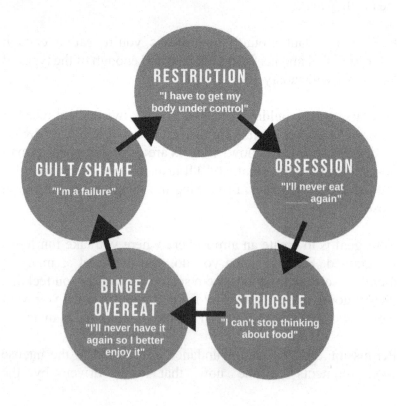

The cycle tends to start with restriction. This restriction can be triggered by many things – a glimpse of your body in the mirror, a bad day or weekend of eating, or panic that swimsuit season is coming. Whatever the situation, you feel a sense of discomfort, and you turn to getting your diet under control and use restriction and deprivation as tools to feel better. Unfortunately, that sets the binge/restrict cycle in motion.

Restriction then leads to obsession. The obsession phase is highlighted by a strong feeling of "I'll never eat ___ again!" There could even be a feeling of confidence behind it if the restriction is leading to some weight loss. During this time, most people are obsessively counting calories and demonizing certain foods or even entire food groups as the cause of all their (or the world's) problems. In essence, you're waging a war against food, and it might even feel like you're winning, for now.

That's when the inevitable struggle phase comes in. You didn't realize it at the time, but you were riding a wave of heightened willpower. But like most willpower dependent diet culture strategies, it eventually wears off. And that's when the inconsistency and struggle start to happen. You start feeling the side effects of the restriction (quantity cravings) and deprivation (quality cravings). You're thinking about food all the time. Those foods you placed off limits are calling out to you, and it's getting harder to keep saying no to them. You might also be feeling hungrier than usual – making it harder to adhere to the arbitrary calorie budget you set for yourself.

That leads to the next phase – bingeing or overeating. You start to rationalize and bargain with yourself in order to eat what you really want. You might just have a bite or a little bit of that food you weren't supposed to have. But that leads to the last supper mentality, which is characterized by thinking you should go ahead and enjoy it now since you aren't supposed to or can't have it again. Unfortunately, the restriction and deprivation spring is wound so tight, that there's a need for a release. Your psychology and physiology then take over, and you end up overeating. The degree to which you overeat is directly correlated to the degree in which you restrict and deprive. The larger and longer the restriction, the larger and longer the overeating. All that restriction and deprivation debt you created now needs to be paid back with interest.

Which leads to feelings of guilt and shame – the final phase of the binge/restrict cycle. This is where you have thoughts of failure. You've overeaten yet again. And you see yourself in the mirror and don't like what you see. And if you recall, this is what starts the binge/restrict cycle all over again with restriction in order to get things under control.

The cycle is rooted in the overvaluing of food, which is valued in direct proportion to how much you've restricted and deprived yourself. The more the restriction and deprivation, the greater the value. Which makes it harder to stop eating once you've started because there is such a high pleasure response to eating something with such high value.

That's the cycle. It's common and it's predictable. In its simplest of forms, it's a period of mindless and out of control eating, followed by a period of intentional restriction to make up for the unwanted behaviors you just engaged in. This restriction then fuels the overeating, and the cycle persists.

The cycle tends to happen on shorter time scales, say via the daytime/nighttime eating cycle, when you restrict and eat well all day only to overeat at night. Or it might be more medium-term, such as the weekday/weekend cycle, when you restrict and are "perfect" all week, only to overeat on the weekend. Or the cycle might be longer in nature. This tends to correlate with the diet cycle when you diet for a few weeks or even months, only to eventually overeat and wipe out all your progress in a fraction of the time.

Whatever the case, recognizing when you're in it is key to getting out of it and staying out of it in the future. If you feel like you need more willpower and discipline with your diet, it's most likely because you really need less restriction and deprivation. This is a good sign that you're about to enter the binge/restrict cycle. Instead of being reactionary, be investigative. Try to understand what part of your relationship with food (or body, exercise, or mind) is creating this unwanted behavior and then go heal it. Address the struggle at the source instead of masking over it with dieting and body control.

Food Labels Matter

How we label our food matters. Labels are loaded with meaning, and meaning influences how we think, feel, and act.

I could call pizza "unhealthy food," "junk food," "fatty food," "fun food," or a "cheat meal," and even though every single label is referring to the same thing, each one will elicit a different feeling in you. Depending on the label, you could feel guilt and shame when you eat the pizza, or you could experience feelings of food freedom. And while you'll be eating the same pizza regardless of the label, what you do after you eat the pizza is determined based on the label and meaning you've attached to your food.

To be fair, even calling pizza "food" is a label. After all, you have to call it something. So it's not about dropping the labels altogether, but rather labeling your food in a way that best produces the feeling and outcome you want.

We see the effects of labels all the time. Marketers carefully choose their words because they want you to feel a certain way. They understand that this feeling produces an action they want. And more times than not, a food label takes the power away from you and gives it to the food.

Would you rather buy a certified pre-owned car or a used car? For all intents and purposes, they are the same thing, but there's a good chance a "pre-owned" car sounds and feels a little more luxurious to you. And because of that, you're going to be much more likely to purchase a "pre-owned" vehicle than you are to shop at the used car lot.

Politicians do this all the time when they want to influence people. "Minimum wage" vs. "living wage." "Stimulus checks" vs. "government handouts." Depending on who you are, these labels create different emotions, which will influence different actions.

So when it comes to your food, you have to become your own food marketer. You have to first be aware of the labels you are attaching to your food, and then you have to pay attention to how each particular label is making you feel and act.

If a label is making you feel guilt or shame over what you eat, it's time you start using more empowering language. Remember, "guilt-free" foods are not foods you eat with certain ingredients – they are foods you eat with a certain attitude. A "guilt-free" food is just something you eat without guilt – aka ALL foods.

So were you "good" with your eating this week? If you weren't "good," what were you? Were you "bad" or were you simply not as consistent as you wanted to be?

Again, the same thing happened, but one label is loaded with feelings of guilt and shame while the other is more objective. And the more objective you can be, the more likely you are to see data simply as feedback to make effective adjustments with, as opposed to spending the next week paying penance for your "bad" eating.

It's up to you to decide how you want to label your food. Each label and its resulting experience is unique to you. Each person's experience depends on their history and the meaning they've attached to that particular label.

Remember, we want to eat in a way that makes us feel our best mentally, emotionally, and physically. That goal isn't just determined based on what we eat. It's also about how we feel when we eat. So choose your labels wisely.

Food Is Not the Enemy

In the car one day, my wife and I were talking to our daughter. She had asked us to buy a particular cereal, and I had said no after reading the label. It had an ingredient that I didn't approve of.

I tried to explain this to her in a way she might understand. I told her, "Did you know there's an ingredient in that cereal they use in embalming fluid?" I thought that would be so disgusting she would say, "OMG, that's gross. I'm never eating that cereal again."

But no, that's not what she said. In fact, she didn't say anything. So, I asked her, "Does that matter to you?" And she said, "Not really. It just tastes sooo good." As we all sat in silence for the next 5 minutes while driving, I sensed there were unspoken thoughts going through all our heads. That's when she spoke – "I can't wait until I'm old enough to move out so I can eat whatever I want."

It was at that moment that I knew we were doing something wrong. The years of preaching about eating healthy food and depriving them of the foods they wanted had created an unhealthy relationship with food.

Our efforts had backfired. The restriction had made her value these foods even more. She wanted what she couldn't have. There was now a forbidden allure to these foods.

While we were making her eat the foods we bought, she was going to her friend's house and eating everything that was off-limits with us. She was also trading lunches with her friends at school to get what she really wanted.

I give this example not to tell you how to raise your own kids, but to illustrate that the same thing happens to us as adults. We deprive ourselves of certain foods in the name of health and weight loss, and then we wonder why we can't resist them. We put these off-limits foods on a pedestal, either worshiping or fearing them.

We tell ourselves we can't eat them. They are bad for us. They will make us fat. They are the enemy. But they are not. An unhealthy relationship with food is what's truly bad for us. An unhealthy relationship with food keeps us from achieving our ideal body. It's this relationship that is the enemy.

When we decide to be healthier or to lose weight, we essentially wage a war against our food. We label various foods as good or bad, healthy or unhealthy. We view calories negatively, and any processed food is seen as resistance against achieving our goals.

Instead of demonizing foods, we need to start seeing the value in them. And I don't just mean whole foods. Everything you eat has value and can potentially meet a need.

But to see the value in your food, you first have to stop seeing it as your enemy. As you continue to heal your relationship with food, you'll find that you naturally gravitate towards foods that make you feel your best, and you're able to eat these foods in an effortless way. And this all happens from a place of unconditional permission.

CHAPTER 3

INTENTIONAL EATING

Meeting Your Needs of the Moment

Back in college was when I first started getting serious about my nutrition. Before that, food and eating just kind of happened on autopilot in the background of my life. When I was hungry, I ate. When I wanted a snack, I'd have a snack. Sometimes the food was more stereotypically healthy and other times it wasn't. But I never felt bad about what I was eating, nor did I ever concern myself with what it was doing to my body.

That attitude towards food didn't stop me from being fit and healthy. Yes, I was just a teenager, but the point is that my food problems didn't start until I decided to get serious and more focused with my eating and body and trying to make them "better".

The only problem is that in the process of being more intentional with my eating, I created a dysfunctional relationship with food. Food became a means to an end – a tool to manipulate my body.

In a way, the idea that I can use food to create the body I want is very exciting. It feels very empowering. You can control your appearance simply by manipulating what, when, and how much you eat.

But that wasn't exactly what happened. Instead, my obsessive focus on what food would do to my body created an unhealthy relationship with food, and I spent the next 20 years yo-yo dieting, living with a binge eating disorder, and hating the way I looked. Not exactly empowering, now is it?

When I made the decision to ditch Diet Culture I needed to retrain myself on my approach to eating. My focus had always been on how much I was supposed to eat, or what kind of foods to eat, or even when to eat them.

But what I really needed was to address WHY I was even eating. My why was always to control my body. And by extension, food allowed me to feel more valuable in society, have more confidence, and be a better person. Or at least that's what I had hoped would happen. It didn't.

So my why needed to change. No longer was I going to use food as a means to an end – a way to control my body and worth. Instead, I was going to start eating in a way that allowed me to mentally, emotionally, and physically feel my best right now – not some day in the future.

I stopped focusing on calories and meal timing and restrictive eating, and instead turned my attention to 3 variables that would meet my needs of the now – satiate, satisfy, and nourish.

When you choose what to eat, how much to eat, and when to eat based on those three variables, you're honoring your needs of the now instead of your desires of the future, which creates less anxiety and obsession surrounding food.

And here's the most important thing – focusing on meeting your needs of the now instead of your desires of the future doesn't mean you're giving up on your goals. Quite the opposite. Your desired future is simply the natural side effect of you consistently meeting your needs of the now. And Intentional

Eating gives you the necessary immediate feedback to make that happen.

Using food to control your future didn't result in the future you wanted. And the reason why is because you were ignoring your needs of the now. By meeting your needs of the now, by choosing foods that satiate, satisfy, and nourish, you consistently string together the necessary number of days of optimal eating that lead to desirable outcomes.

Satiate, Satisfy, Nourish

Getting intentional with your eating doesn't mean focusing on using food to manipulate your body. It means that in any given moment, you're choosing foods that satiate, satisfy, and nourish you so you can feel your best right now.

Honoring your needs of the now is key to realizing the benefits of the future. But understand that these future benefits, like improved health and fitness, are secondary to the primary benefit of feeling the best you can in any given moment.

You might think that eating whole foods 100% of the time is the goal, but it's not. The goal is to satiate, satisfy, and nourish the best you can given the circumstances of the moment. And that's important to understand, because your needs of the moment are not static – they are constantly changing based on what's going on in your life.

What is satiating right now might not be so satiating tomorrow or next week or even later in the day. What's satisfying now might be what you'd consider a stereotypically whole food, but it might also be a cookie. And the best nourishment you could give yourself right now might be different than what you could give yourself at another time.

Your needs must be addressed in a way that honors the variability of the moment. If you try to eat nothing but whole foods because you think that's the most satiating, satisfying, and nourishing thing you could theoretically eat, then you run the risk of falling short of meeting your needs of the moment. You might need something more satisfying right now, or a bigger meal than usual. And if you choose to eat based on whether a food is healthy or not rather than if it meets your needs of the moment, you can create a state of restriction and deprivation. This can lead to unfavorable side effects in the future – like inconsistent eating, falling into the binge/restrict cycle, nighttime and weekend overeating, or emotional eating.

So let's take a look at these three variables a bit closer:

Satiation is a food's or meal's ability to fulfill your physical hunger. More times than not, a stereotypically healthy food or meal will satiate you better than processed foods simply because of the sheer volume they have per calorie. This fills you up and does a good job of keeping you satiated for 3-4 hours or longer at times.

However, what's most satiating for you in any given moment will differ. Satiation isn't just about protein, fiber, and food volume. Other factors influence satiety too. All things being equal, a more satisfying meal will tend to be more satiating than a meal of equal size that's less satisfying.

In addition, eating beyond a comfortable level of satiation doesn't make a meal more satiating. If you end up feeling physically or even mentally uncomfortable because you ate too much, that's not optimal satiation. So sometimes, eating less is the way to improve satiation.

So how are you supposed to know what to eat then? You make your best guess, have an eating experience, assess the results, and then iterate. No one gets everything right the first time. True progress comes from trying things and making improvements on behaviors over time. So if you eat too much, then you know a slight adjustment needs to be made for next time. Over time, you start to understand your body and needs better, and you'll eat more intuitively.

This contrasts with the usual way of eating. Typically we set calorie intakes and determine food choices based on whether they will help us lose weight. We don't view our eating through the lens of satiate, satisfy, and nourish. So we're eating mindlessly in that respect. But when you place the eating lens where it needs to be, consecutive eating experiences are more productive, and you're able to anchor these subjective variables and iterate.

Satisfaction is the next Intentional Eating variable. It addresses your mental hunger, also known as cravings, desires, wants, or enjoyment.

This is the variable most people ignore when they diet. There's a belief that satisfaction needs to be sacrificed in order to achieve your goals. This is wrong. It's the sacrificing of satisfaction that leads to unmet goals. Your diet must be satisfying or you'll face consistency issues.

Most people think of satisfaction simply as what tastes good. Yes, that is one variable that affects satisfaction, but there are many more, and you should experiment with all of them to get the most out of your diet. Besides taste, the texture of your food affects satisfaction. The same food prepared different ways can be more or less enjoyable. A baked potato and mashed potatoes are both the same potato, but they have different textures, and most people will find one more satisfying than the other.

Temperature is another variable. Food or liquids that are hot, cold, or room temperature can all affect satisfaction differently.

Meal variety matters too. Depending on the person, having similar meals day-to-day might be more satisfying than different ones most days, and vice versa.

The presentation and environment you eat in is another variable. Eating the same meal at home around screaming kids will have a different satisfaction level than that meal in a 5-star restaurant with dim lighting and soft background music.

The nutrition of a meal can also affect satisfaction. So can nostalgic attachments to foods. The list goes on and on. You need to consider these factors and experiment with your food until you find a dozen or so go-to meals that best satiate, satisfy, and nourish you.

Lastly, Nourishment. Nourishment addresses the nutritional makeup of your food. It's about your food's ability to provide energy for physical activity, nutrients for health, and fuel for your mind to think and maintain a positive and productive attitude. Everything from calories, protein, carbs, fats, vitamins, minerals, and antioxidants are needed by the body and mind at any given moment to feel and function at its best.

Like satiation, nourishment is usually best met through whole foods because they have more nutrients per calorie. But not every meal has to be perfectly nutritious every time you eat. The goal is to do your best meeting your needs of the moment.

There will be times when you actually crave the nutrition of a salad. I feel this way any time I'm coming back from a vacation where I found it more difficult to eat well. When I get home I'm craving my smoothie, and it's one of the first things I'll have regardless of what time it is.

But other times you might need to prioritize satiation or satisfaction. Remember, your diet isn't just about any one particular meal. While you absolutely should assess and honor your needs of the moment, if you zoom out a little and look at your eating over the course of a week or a month, you want to be able to say that yes – overall I satiated, satisfied, and nourished my body well and feel the best I can given the circumstances.

There Are No Empty Calories

Diet culture teaches you that there is this thing called "empty calories."

That wine you drank. That cake you ate. That bowl of cereal you had.

You've been led to believe these things are empty calories because they contain few nutrients. But who says nutrients are the be-all-end-all yardstick for your food?

If that was the only thing that mattered, then our grocery stores would be filled with nothing but nutrient-dense fruits and vegetables. Restaurants wouldn't be a thing (why go out when you can eat the same thing at home?). And family get-togethers and holidays like Thanksgiving wouldn't revolve around food.

Yet all these things do exist. Why? Because food serves a purpose outside of just fuel.

Food also meets cultural, societal, social, mental, emotional, and yes – physical needs.

So, empty calories? They don't exist. Everything you eat fulfills a current need in your life.

You can't pigeonhole food based on its nutritional content. Doing so blinds you to understanding why you are drawn to eating certain foods.

Yes, of course, certain foods have more nutrients than others. No one is going to argue that. A 500-calorie muffin is going to have fewer vitamins and minerals than a serving of broccoli. But that's as far as this empty calorie ideology is going to take you.

In reality, there is no such thing as empty calories. Everything you eat or drink is meeting a need of yours.

A glass of wine or that 500-calorie muffin might be void of micronutrients, but it's far from empty nutrition when you consider the psychological nature of eating. And that's the part most people neglect when they are caught up in Diet Culture.

Generally speaking, the majority of people know what foods are most nutritious and would be best for their body. This has never been an issue. I joke around a lot that most people don't need a nutritionist – they need a therapist. We don't need more articles about why you should eat more veggies or that you should eat mostly whole foods. That's nothing mind-blowing.

What we need is more people helping us understand WHY we choose to eat the things we do despite our desires not to eat them. We need a better understanding of our psychology and our relationship with food.

This is what rejecting the idea of empty calories helps you accomplish. It helps you understand the relationship you have with food so that you can heal it. If you just write off foods solely on the basis of whether they have nutrients or not, you're ignoring the unique dynamic your psychology plays in your eating.

Eating isn't a mathematical equation. Nor is it rational the majority of the time. And when you realize that most eating is done on a subconscious/unconscious level, you can begin to understand why calorie tracking apps and cliche sayings about food don't make a dent in your eating struggle.

Intentional eating is about moving beyond the 1+1 nutrition philosophy that Diet Culture teaches, and instead adopting a deeper understanding of all the moving parts that go into why you eat the way you do.

Why did you drink that glass of wine? Why did you eat that muffin? That nutritional decision isn't empty – it's packed full of valuable information. Those calories are full of data points that help you dissect your relationship with food so you can heal and achieve your ideal body.

Did you choose the wine because you were celebrating your birthday with friends? Or did you drink the wine because you were stressed out from work? Diet culture teaches these two glasses of wine as being equal – empty calories. But as I'm sure you can see, they are not empty glasses. Each highlights a different relationship with food – one that might need healing and one that might be just fine.

So, ditch all the cliche sayings, food rules, and disempowering meanings diet culture has attached to food. Its goal is singular – to get you into a smaller body at all costs. Ironically, despite its narrow focus, it's highly ineffective at doing that. Instead, understand that all food is meeting a need, and that your journey is one of personal discovery, understanding, and healing. All food is full of valuable information, and ditching Diet Culture will allow you to see it.

Flexible Structure

There's a very big misconception that when you ditch Diet Culture, stop counting calories, and give yourself full unconditional permission to eat what you want, that there's no longer any structure to your eating. People visualize this big intuitive eating free-for-all where you're flying by the seat of your pants, eating whatever sounds good whenever the mood strikes.

I can assure you that this kind of approach would be hard for anyone to follow. Humans need structure to thrive. We are habitual creatures. Structure prevents decision fatigue and makes it easier to create consistency.

But there's one big problem – Diet Culture's version of structure isn't what we want. Its version is very similar to a rigid meal plan where you are eating a specific thing at a specific time, all planned well in advance, and there's zero veering from the plan. If you do, you failed.

That is not the kind of structure we want. We need something that gives us guidance, yet also allows for our unique needs and circumstances. That's where flexible structure comes into play.

Flexible structure allows you to have a framework to build and iterate upon. It helps you to plan for eating decisions ahead of time, but allows you to make in-the-moment changes in order to account for changing needs. And then your structure adapts to your unique life situation over time until you have a very personalized way of eating. Call it the "Me-Diet".

What we advise our members and clients to do is plan their days with a series of core meals and hunger snacks. We start off with 3 core meals – usually a breakfast, lunch, and dinner, as most people are able to utilize that structure regardless of their life circumstances. If you have a job, you can usually eat before going to work, when you get home, and sometime while you're there on a break.

The important thing to remember here is that this is only a starting point. It's a way of guiding your intuitiveness. Over time you might realize that less or more meals each day is ideal for you. I personally have 4 meals. Sometimes that turns into 3 meals and a snack when I'm less active and am more easily satiated on less food.

In between these core meals, you have hunger snacks. These snacks are not required. They are tools used to get you to your next core meal without you arriving at that meal feeling ravenous. Some people need something between lunch and dinner. And some people need or enjoy having something in the evening or at night too.

Plan your core meals out so they meet your needs. They should satiate, satisfy, and nourish. Getting in those 3 core meals meeting those 3 variables will really help move you through your day with ease.

If a meal comes up and it's clear to you that what you have planned to eat isn't going to meet those needs of the moment, then you are flexible and eat what will honor them. Your needs of the moment are always the priority. The planning and structure just make this process easier.

Over time you might realize that one of your core meals needs to be smaller or bigger based on satiation levels you're achieving, or they might need more satisfaction or nourishment. So what do you do? You iterate on your meal and adjust it to ensure satiation, satisfaction, and nutrition are as optimized as possible. This is what's going to keep you from feeling restricted and deprived, which will keep you as consistent as possible.

You might also realize that your afternoon hunger snack just isn't enough food to carry you over to dinner. That has been me. So that snack became a meal. That's what I needed to feel satiated, satisfied, and nourished at that particular time. Your needs will be different than mine. But the structure will help you understand your unique needs.

Think of flexible structure as a sort of living document. It's constantly in flux depending on what's going on in your life. You will end up gravitating towards a certain structure. For example, many people find they aren't that hungry first thing in the morning, so they won't have their first meal until mid to late morning. Others will need a different number of core meals. Others will get hungry later after dinner and will need either a hunger snack or a full meal. Your unique satiation, satisfaction, and nourishment needs will determine what your flexible structure looks like.

So start with your 3 core meals. Use hunger snacks in between these meals to ensure you begin eating your core meals at productive hunger levels. And then iterate on your structure until you have a plan that works for you.

What's Healthy Anyways?

One of the biggest objections people have to the idea of honoring their satisfaction needs, and at times eating fun foods to do that, is that it isn't healthy for you. After all, how could eating things like pizza, ice cream, cookies, and candy be healthy?

I understand this objection. I once held this belief too. But all it did was keep me in the binge/restrict cycle – constantly trying to be perfect by eating all whole foods, and then unintentionally breaking that perfection with periods of eating all the foods I was placing off limits.

This idea of labeling foods as healthy and unhealthy is deeply rooted in isolationist nutrition thinking. What that means is we tend to compare foods in isolation in order to make a determination of whether it's healthy for us or not. Not to mention, "healthy" and "nutritious" are not synonyms. What is nutritious is more objective and absolute. It either has a lot of nutrients or it doesn't. But what is healthy, as you will soon see, is much more subjective and relative to each individual person.

For example, when you compare an apple to a cupcake, I don't think anyone is going to argue that the apple isn't more nutritious than the cupcake. It's a whole food, has fiber, nutrients, and antioxidants. The cupcake is mostly sugar, flour, and fat.

So yes… in isolation, the apple is healthier and more nutritious than the cupcake. The problem with this thinking is that we don't eat foods in isolation. Nor does food just sit on a shelf and get looked at and analyzed. It has to be consumed by people. And people have different operating systems. We all have different psychology, goals, genetics, and circumstances. And these are what actually dictate whether something is healthy for YOU.

In addition, everything we eat influences every other thing that we eat. Our eating is a lifestyle, and that lifestyle is made up of hundreds of meals that all influence one another. When you eat that apple, it creates physiological and psychological changes that will influence when you eat next, what you eat next, and how much you will eat. The same goes for the cupcake.

If you say no to the cupcake and instead opt for the apple simply because "it's healthier" based on isolationist nutrition thinking, it is entirely possible that choice is creating feelings of deprivation that sets you up for a compulsion to eat that cupcake later.

And what normally happens is you don't just have one cupcake, you have multiple cupcakes – sometimes spanning days or even weeks. You basically end up paying back the deprivation debt you created plus interest.

If foregoing the cupcake and eating an apple instead leads to you feeling out of control and bingeing on a bunch of foods that make you feel horrible, is the apple really healthy for you? Does it lead to a healthy outcome?

What if deciding to eat the cupcake lowers your feelings of deprivation and intensity around fun foods later? What if the weekend comes and you don't feel that upward pressure on your eating and desire to let go and live a little? What if you end up eating consistently through the weekend instead of bingeing on thousands of calories?

Would you say the cupcake was the better choice over the apple? Did the cupcake lead to the healthier outcome in the end?

Food cannot be looked at in isolation. There is a cause and effect to every eating decision you make. The healthiest decision to make right now is the one that will lead to the healthiest outcome later. And this healthy outcome is a byproduct of you understanding and honoring your body's need for satiation, satisfaction, and nourishment of the moment – instead of a generic "healthy" or "not healthy" food label.

What this means is you have to start looking at your diet as a whole. You have to zoom out a bit and see the big picture. You have to start judging what's healthy for you, not based on a side by side comparison of the individual foods we eat, but by the overall outcomes in which they create.

You can start to see now how the whole "what's healthy" question is more complicated than what it seems. Nobody lives in a lab where all our food is provided for us and we have no option to eat anything else besides what's given to us.

We live in the real world with real life dynamics. We have social gatherings, holidays, temptations, and cultural pressures we have to manage on a daily basis. And frankly, sometimes we just want to have fun with food – and that's OK!

CHAPTER 4

EMOTIONAL EATING

The Perfect Storm

It was 2pm on a Monday. I had eaten perfectly up until then, but I could feel the pressure building to have a fun night with some mindless TV and junk food.

As the afternoon went on, I could feel a pull towards food and letting go a little and enjoying myself. By the time dinner arrived, I had decided to make a trip to the grocery store.

I got a frozen pizza, a half gallon of cookies and cream ice cream, and a big bag of jelly beans. When I got home, I started eating my way through all the food. I was full after 3/4 of the pizza. I was stuffed after eating half the ice cream. And I felt physically sick by the time I had finished the jelly beans.

As I was eating all this food, I felt physically and emotionally horrible. I felt guilty. I felt ashamed. I felt frustrated. I promised myself as I was eating that this would be the last time I binged – that tomorrow I would start over and eat my planned meals. It's easy to make that promise when you're stuffing your face. But it's even easier to say "one last time" when you really want to eat something you think you shouldn't.

I wish I could say this was an isolated event. But this day had unfolded the same way every day for the last month. Every day I would start with the best of intentions only to feel a pull towards a nighttime binge. I'd promise to be better tomorrow. And the cycle would continue.

I'd eat upwards of 7-8 thousand calories a night and gain a pound a day for an entire month. By the time a month had passed and 30 pounds had been put on, the pain had finally reached a critical point that changes needed to happen. But even still, the random nighttime, weekend, or 30-day binges would occur.

You might not have a binge eating disorder like I did, although it's much more common than people realize. Instead, most people have a similar issue, but to a lesser degree. This is known as emotional eating.

My bingeing started when I was in college when I first dove into bodybuilding culture. Suddenly, food went from something I didn't think much about, straight to it being a tool to control my body.

So, I restricted calories and deprived myself of enjoyable foods by trying my best to eat a 100% whole foods diet. Because I didn't think there was any way I could lose weight eating sugar, pizza, or any other stereotypical junk food.

The restriction and deprivation would build throughout the week, and it would culminate into a weekend binge. At the time, we called these days "cheat days", which meant we just planned to eat whatever we wanted. It would kind of work since the other days had low enough calories that we could "afford" to be free on the weekend.

So began my binge eating. And many people are simply stuck right there. They purposely restrict and deprive themselves in an effort to control their body, and they create a slingshot-like effect that leads to nighttime, weekend, or occasional periods of out of control eating. It might not be a full out binge, but it's mindlessly overeating in an out of control way.

In time, these binge episodes provided something else – an escape from the struggles of life and the uncomfortable emotions that were a part of it. It wasn't something I was conscious of. All I knew was I was eating foods I didn't want to be eating, and eating them in quantities that were more than desirable.

But subconsciously, I was driven to these emotional eating episodes because they made me feel present. When I was eating, the depression of my past and anxieties of my future would temporarily go away. And the more I tried to smother and not feel the uncomfortable feelings stemming from my life, the more I would use food at night or on the weekends to cope.

And this is where most people are stuck with emotional eating. They have the perfect storm brewing. They have underlying physiological pressures because of purposeful caloric restriction and food satisfaction deprivation in order to control their body and self-worth. And that is combined with ineffective coping strategies when it comes to the perfectly natural but uncomfortable feelings they have.

Whatever coping strategy you use, the first part of the solution will always be the same – you have to learn to feel your feelings instead of trying to pretend like they aren't there. You have to change the relationship you have with your emotions and stop smothering them any time you feel discomfort. When you do this, you're able to get down to the root of your emotional eating struggle and address it at the source.

Sitting With Your Emotions

We've been conditioned to believe that emotions are either good or bad. Emotions like frustration, stress, anxiety, anger, and jealousy are seen as bad. And emotions like happiness, joy, love, and gratitude are considered good.

But like most of the things we've talked about, we only believe these things because of the meaning we've attached to them. An emotion is just an emotion. It is a signal from your body. It's the beliefs we have about them that determine whether we think they are good or bad.

All emotions are good. Stress, anger, frustration – these are gifts in the sense that your body is showing you what you need to work on to feel in alignment. They only become bad emotions when you internalize the discomfort and let it become your identity.

If you can be self-aware enough to recognize what you are feeling, you can observe the discomfort, label it, and use it as a clue for getting down to the root of the emotion that is creating the pain.

But that's the problem. These so-called negative emotions are uncomfortable. So we do everything we can to fight them, cover them up, and pretend like they don't exist.

At the first signs of discomfort, we reach for our coping strategies. And for most people, food is high up on their list of coping tools. It's one of the most accessible and socially acceptable ways of coping with life's discomfort.

Others might turn to alcohol, drugs, sex, shopping, codependency, arguing – nearly anything you can imagine. These are maladaptive coping strategies. In other words, they help you deal with the discomfort, but they create a secondary problem in the process.

Sometimes we even preempt the feelings of discomfort. We are so aware of the patterns of life that make us feel bad that we subconsciously get ahead of the problem by coping with an emotion that hasn't even manifested yet.

But despite the discomfort with the emotions you feel, you have to get used to sitting with that discomfort instead of running to smother it at the first hint of it emerging.

We do this by changing our relationship with our emotions. As I said before, emotions, whether they are stereotypically good or bad, are simply signals from your body that its needs are either being met or they are not.

Sitting with the discomfort allows you to identify this emotion and its underlying unmet need. It helps you solve the problem by addressing the root cause of the discomfort, instead of covering it up with food and creating a secondary problem. The latter throws you into a downward spiral that strengthens each time you feel the emotion, while the former allows you to fix the problem by making yourself whole again.

Your goal when you feel the pull to reach for food to cope is to pause. Sit with the discomfort. Identify the emotion you're feeling. And then determine which one of your underlying needs isn't being met.

Interestingly enough, most people who sit with the discomfort report that the feeling dissipates on its own in time. And in the process, they weaken the grip the emotion has on them because they are no longer afraid of feeling it. As the feeling comes up in the future, it passes through them instead of them latching onto it and internalizing it. They no longer become the feeling. They just recognize it, acknowledge it, and use it as a tool for personal growth.

Facing Your Problems Head On

One day, I really decided to tackle not just my binge eating struggle, but also my marijuana addiction and every other maladaptive coping strategy I was using to deal with the uncomfortable feelings of my life.

This wasn't the first time I had tried to quit these things. Like most people, I've tried to quit bad habits over and over again, only to go right back to these coping strategies when things inevitably got hard.

Something I noticed was that every time I tried to quit a bad habit, my life suddenly seemed to get more difficult. Without fail, I'd go into this process with the best of intentions, and then life would throw all kinds of problems at me. Financial struggles would pop up. The kids would have issues to deal with. Work would get stressful.

So I'd rationalize that now was not the best time to work on this stuff. Giving up my coping strategies, even though they were causing me harm, was more painful than overcoming the problem itself.

But all this changed one day when I had one of my biggest breakthroughs ever. I had been seeing my situation and struggle incorrectly all along. Here I was thinking that by some random chance, my life was always getting more difficult the moment I decided to do the work and quit my negative coping strategies.

I thought that life was just picking on me and was deciding these were perfect times to go ahead and throw some big problems at me. I thought I was the victim – thinking, "why me and why now?"

When I saw the truth, it changed my life. The truth is I didn't suddenly start having problems the moment I addressed my emotional eating and stopped coping using food. I wasn't the recipient of some timed plot by the universe to make my life difficult the moment I wanted to get better.

What I realized was that these problems I was suddenly experiencing? They had always been there. I just didn't see or feel them because I was stuffing them down using food, drugs, and other behaviors. When I removed these coping strategies, my blinders and emotional dampeners came off, and I suddenly felt and experienced all the problems I had been ignoring all that time.

Recognizing this, the next time my uncomfortable feelings came up, I didn't run to food. I didn't run to pot or alcohol or any other of my usual tools. I just sat with them. I sat with the discomfort. I felt.

Was it painful? Of course it was. I had become extremely sensitized to discomfort from all the years using these coping strategies. But I sat with the discomfort anyways. And in doing so, I learned about myself, what it was I was really needing, and healed.

Look… you might not have a binge eating disorder. And you might not have a struggle with substances either. But most people do have something they rely on to cope with the uncomfortable feelings of life. And rarely are these coping strategies healthy for you.

Emotional eating comes in many shapes and sizes. But it's rooted in using food to cope with discomfort. So the solution is always going to be the same – sit with the discomfort, identify your emotions, explore your underlying needs that are currently being unproductively met using food, and work towards meeting them directly. When you do that, your actual problems get solved, and there's no discomfort to even deal with. You addressed the problem at its source instead of slapping band-aids on it using coping tools.

Your Unmet Needs

Emotional eating is a form of addiction. That statement will be denied by a lot of people – professionals included. But I continue to argue my case.

They will say that you can't be addicted to something (food) that you need to survive. The only problem here is I'm not talking about a physical addiction. While food most definitely creates a physiological pleasure response, and some foods and people have this response more than others, I don't necessarily think of this as addiction.

But if we're being technical here, I could argue that everyone is physically addicted to food. After all, what happens when you try to abstain from food? Your body's chemistry changes, you go through a form of withdrawal, food-seeking behaviors increase, and you eventually eat. Call it what you want – a physical dependency, maybe. The point is, food has power and influence.

However, my case for emotional eating being an addiction has more to do with it being a psychological addiction. It is a maladaptive coping strategy to an underlying unmet need. And when you keep coming back to food time and time again knowing it's hurting you, can't help yourself, and can't stop when you want to – well... that's an addiction.

Addiction comes in many shapes and sizes. It has different degrees of intensity. But it comes down to someone engaging in behaviors that feel out of their control in order to cope with emotional discomfort resulting from underlying unmet needs.

Emotional eating might be your current go-to strategy for coping with discomfort, but these psychological addictions can literally take the form of anything – shopping, gambling, sex, alcohol, drugs, dieting, exercise, arguing, co-dependency, biting pencils... literally anything you can imagine.

None of these things are necessarily bad in isolation. But when they become patterns, and they create secondary problems in your life, and you can't stop, then you have a psychological addiction.

Why is this important? Because if you understand this is the root of your emotional eating struggle, you can start addressing the problem effectively. You will stop using surface-level calorie restriction in an attempt to control the overeating. Because eating less isn't the solution to eating too much. Just like how not drinking isn't a substitute for drinking.

You have to get to the root of the struggle – your underlying unmet needs that are creating the uncomfortable emotions, that are driving the undesirable coping strategy – eating (or whatever coping strategy you're using). Otherwise, if the root problem doesn't get addressed, there will always be pressure to cope.

As human beings, we have needs. These needs have to be met in order for us to survive both physically and psychologically. Unfortunately, many people meet these needs in a destructive way. One, because they don't know how to meet that particular need in a healthy way, and two because they don't even know what the need is. A lifetime of subconscious maladaptive coping has numbed them to their needs.

That's why sitting with the discomfort when you feel the pull to whip out your typical coping strategy is so important. This is what allows you to "see" and feel the emotion and identify the need that is driving the discomfort.

These needs are plentiful and unique to the person. But they could be your need for safety, love, understanding, support, entertainment, self-expression, joy, nature, growth, purpose, creativity, sleep, touch, relief, autonomy, play, challenge, connection, intimacy, or movement.

The list goes on and on. When one or more of these needs isn't being met, we feel emotional discomfort. You might feel upset, depressed, lost, anxious, stressed, sad, mournful, frustrated, agitated, mad, resentful, or even bored.

Most of us weren't raised to effectively handle these emotions, so instead of directly meeting our underlying needs, we cope. Unfortunately, our coping strategies aren't the best either and we reach for what's familiar, easy, accessible, and socially acceptable. Food is an easy solution. And emotional eating takes root.

As you eat, these uncomfortable feelings disappear for a bit. But like with all maladaptive coping strategies, they create secondary problems and also don't solve the first one – meeting your unmet need.

If you just try to stop emotionally eating without meeting the need, then that need will be met elsewhere. It will be channeled into another maladaptive coping strategy. Until you solve the problem at the source, you will always be reactively coping to emotional discomfort.

So sit with the discomfort. Feel the emotion. Identify the underlying unmet need. And work on addressing it directly. Yes, it might take time to meet this need effectively. You might have a lot of work to do or past trauma to overcome. But once you learn to meet your needs, the drive to cope dissipates, and you live a more fulfilling life experience.

Learning How to Cope

Not all your needs are going to be able to be met right away. Some unmet needs can be fixed in a moment or a day, while others will take time to work towards fulfilling.

You might need to have several conversations with someone in order to work through issues. You might need the assistance of a therapist. You might need time to experiment with ideas in order to find the right behavior that best honors your needs.

The key is to make sure you're at least working towards fulfilling your needs, even if they don't get immediately met. That is the part most people neglect, so they become overly dependent on coping strategies to get them from eating episode to eating episode.

Your approach to emotional eating will require two parallel paths. One is working towards directly meeting your needs. And the other is finding productive coping strategies while you're doing that.

With coping strategies, we have both proactive and reactive types. Most people are focused on reactive coping, also known as what you do after you start feeling emotional discomfort.

And within reactive coping, we have adaptive and maladaptive strategies. Maladaptive would be the strategies that cause secondary problems. This includes emotional eating, but also includes any other behaviors that create secondary problems. On the other hand, adaptive coping strategies will be behaviors that help you self-soothe without making your situation worse. The list of adaptive coping strategies is long, but includes things like going for a walk, calling a friend, seeing a movie, getting a massage, working out, reading a book, deep breathing, etc.

Your job is to experiment with various behaviors until you find one that helps you get through the moment in a productive way, all while remembering that the primary goal is to be working towards meeting your underlying needs so that coping isn't necessary in the first place.

And then you have proactive coping strategies. These are behaviors you bake into your day right now, that better help you manage emotional discomfort later. They are behaviors that build emotional resilience, so that, relatively speaking, similar life situations don't cause you as much discomfort anymore, which results in less of a need to cope.

Proactive coping strategies include things like exercise, sufficient sleep, meditation, or engaging in flow state activities that bring you joy. These behaviors refuel your willpower and make you better equipped to handle life's stressors.

If you combine productive proactive and reactive coping strategies with vigilance in directly meeting your needs, your drive to emotionally eat will be dramatically reduced or even eliminated altogether. At the very least, the frequency and the intensity of the episodes will be greatly diminished, and you will be able to check the box on yet another aspect of healing your relationship with food.

The 3 Forms of Emotional Eating

When people think of emotional eating, they often picture a scenario in which they, or someone else, is feeling stressed, bored, or experiencing another uncomfortable emotion, and they turn to food to soothe themselves. More often than not, they eat more than they'd like, which creates a secondary problem they then have to solve.

While this is absolutely a form of emotional eating, it isn't the only form. There are actually three different types of emotional eating, and most people have experienced all three. Interestingly enough, only two of these are actually problematic. So, let's take a look at all three.

First, we have what I just described – eating to soothe to the point that it creates a secondary problem. You're stressed from a day at work, sit down in front of the TV that night, and eat away your feelings. Unfortunately, you consume more than you needed, and now you're left with another problem – your body.

So you start the next day off dieting, hoping to make up for the mistake you made the previous night. But this worry about your body and gaining weight only stresses you out more, leading to more emotional eating. You find yourself in a downward spiral and struggle to escape it.

Your approach to overcoming this form of emotional eating was what I outlined earlier in this chapter. You sit with the discomfort to feel your emotions, then identify and address your underlying unmet needs causing these uncomfortable emotions. Concurrently, you engage in more productive coping strategies (both proactive and reactive).

The second form of emotional eating is when you use food to soothe, yet it doesn't create a secondary problem. That's right... not all forms of emotional eating are detrimental! Food is one of many tools you can use to regulate your nervous system (one of its primary purposes), and if it helps you without creating more problems, it's a productive form of emotional eating.

I once had a client struggling with emotional eating. Every night she indulged in chocolate and felt immense guilt afterward. We worked on overcoming her challenge for a long time, but we didn't have much luck.

As her coach, this was my fault. Not because I couldn't help her overcome her emotional eating struggle, but because I made a huge assumption – presuming her emotional eating was problematic in the first place.

During a random coaching call, new information emerged. Here I was thinking she was digging into heaps of chocolate and making herself sick. But in reality, she was only eating 1-2 small squares of a chocolate bar!

I was blown away, as I had been projecting my personal experiences with emotional eating and bingeing, assuming others overindulged to the point of discomfort. But she wasn't. She was only consuming around 50 calories of dark chocolate each evening.

That was the first time it really clicked that not all emotional eating was bad. Sometimes, it's even beneficial. If a modest 50-calorie investment helps you regulate your nervous system without causing additional problems, then that's a useful way of eating.

I use a similar approach every night, enjoying a 100-calorie Greek yogurt cookies and cream bar or a small bowl of cereal. I'm not always hungry, but I enjoy having something as I unwind from the day and watch TV. This routine serves as a helpful form of emotional eating for me, regulating my nervous system, promoting consistency, and enhancing my overall life experience.

And finally, we have our third form of emotional eating, which I call "emotional non-eating." When people are feeling overwhelming emotions, one of two things usually happens – they either eat to soothe, or they don't eat much at all. This latter behavior is still emotional eating because you are eating in an emotional way that is out of alignment with your body's needs.

That's what all unproductive forms of emotional eating have in common – you don't eat in a way that meets your body's needs, and it leads to a secondary problem.

Now, this form of emotional eating can be particularly difficult to overcome. When you lose your appetite because of life struggles, it can be hard to force yourself to eat. The framework I outlined above still applies. However, it's also going to take some gentle reminding that taking care of yourself by eating in a way that satiates, satisfies, and nourishes you will help you best deal with whatever life is currently throwing at you. In the meantime, a great deal of self-compassion needs to be part of the equation.

This is an unintentional form of emotional non-eating. Very rarely do we just decide to not eat. It's usually because of great loss or pain that we lose our appetite. However, we also undergo intentional forms of emotional non-eating. And this is best known as dieting.

In an effort to distract ourselves from some of the pains we're feeling in our life, or to feel a sense of control, many people take up dieting. Obviously, dieting isn't a form of overeating – at least not in the short term. It usually does lead to a cause and effect scenario of restriction and then overeating later though. But in the short-term, we try to make ourselves feel better by restricting calories and depriving ourselves of satisfaction in our diet.

Dieting does not meet your needs. It doesn't meet the needs of your life that you're attempting to mask over, nor does it meet your nutritional needs. Dieting attempts to indirectly make your problems better by controlling the shape of your body, which doesn't work.

The solution? You continue working towards ditching Diet Culture and you plug yourself into the Ideal Body Formula™. And while you do that, you work through the emotional eating framework of sitting with your emotions, identifying and addressing your unmet needs, and finding productive ways to cope.

PART II:

RELATIONSHIP WITH BODY

CHAPTER 5

SELF-CONNECTION

Ditch the Scale

Weighing myself every morning (and sometimes night) was a daily ritual. It's what I thought I needed to do in order to lose weight. After all, how was I supposed to know if I was losing weight if I wasn't weighing myself?

Like many people, I lost weight using the scale. And I tended to gain weight when I wasn't weighing myself. This experience reinforced the belief that the scale was a necessary asset on my journey. But this thinking was misguided. I was confusing correlation with causation, and I was selectively choosing my evidence – completely ignoring the fact that when I wasn't weighing myself, I simply just wasn't taking care of myself.

I treated the act of weighing or not weighing myself as the cause of my success or failure, when in reality, these outcomes were just side effects of my thoughts and behaviors at the time. When I was being consistent, I just so happened to also be weighing myself. And when I wasn't, I was hiding from the scale – afraid to see (or not caring about) what my weight was doing.

Not weighing myself didn't cause me to gain weight. I simply stopped weighing myself whenever I wasn't getting the results I wanted. And I wasn't getting the results I wanted because I was stuck in Diet Culture, making all my healthy behaviors contingent upon whether they made the number on the scale go down. So if you're going to credit the scale for your success, you better also blame it for your failures. Because the unwanted behaviors that led to you not weighing yourself anymore were the side effect of you engaging in Diet Culture behaviors in the first place.

When you use food as a tool for controlling the scale, and you exercise for the purpose of body manipulation, it's only a matter of time before you experience the side effects. Hiding from the scale is the consequence of using it in the first place. These behaviors are flip sides of the same coin.

The good news is that the scale is not necessary for you to mentally, emotionally, and physically feel your best. In fact, the opposite is usually true – most people who weigh themselves frequently have struggled with their bodies for most of their life. And in the majority of these cases, the scale is actually creating more harm than good.

How many times have you stepped on the scale and seen a higher than expected number and let it upset you? Either you see that number and question what the point in all your hard work is, or you decide to double down on the restriction and deprivation you've already been engaging in, which just exacerbates the issue and keeps you stuck.

Or you see a lower than expected number, are elated, and proceed to rationalize that you have room to "have fun" and relax a little with your diet. Had you not weighed yourself, you would've continued to engage in behaviors that made you feel your best. But now that you think you have room to relax, you're more likely to act in a way that takes you out of alignment with feeling your best and takes you further from your ideal body.

It's not the scale's fault. It accurately does what it's supposed to do. The problem is your relationship with the scale. Specifically, it's the meaning you've attached to weight, and your belief that your weight needs to be managed. And if you really think about it, it's not your weight you've been trying to manage all along – it's how you feel about yourself that you've been trying to control. So the scale just ends up applying this constant force to your emotional strings.

Your weight does not need managing. Remember, your ideal body is a natural side effect of healthy relationships with food, body, exercise, and mind. Side effects happen from causes. So it's the causes you need to focus on and manage. And when it comes to transformation, the causes are your thoughts and behaviors.

Your weight is not a thought. It is not a behavior. So it's not something that's in your direct control. If it were, you might actually be able to manage it. But it's not. So any attempt to directly manage it usually leaves you frustrated, as your weight is several steps removed from your direct influence.

The empowering thoughts and behaviors that create your desired outcomes are best identified when you're in a state of self-connection and awareness. And ditching the scale on your terms is what results in you achieving this state. When you intentionally get rid of the scale, you are forced to turn inwards and start listening to your body. You get more in tune with what it really needs to thrive. You trust your body to tell you what to do instead of relying on the scale to do that for you.

That might sound utopian to you, but your body can guide you with accuracy better than any external tool can. After all, why wouldn't it be more accurate? You're literally going right to the source and addressing its needs directly. The scale will never be able to do that for you. In fact, not only is the scale not in tune with your body, but it takes you further from self-connection – driving a wedge between you and your body's needs.

The scale in and of itself isn't good or bad. It can be used successfully as a tool to achieve specific goals, but not until after you have healed and have a healthy relationship with your body. If you try to use the scale while you have an unhealthy relationship with your body, it's like staying in a toxic relationship while you're trying to heal.

So long as weight remains a barometer for your self-worth, health, and happiness, you will always be honoring the scale over your body's needs. It'll keep you future focused and seeing food and exercise as a means to an end, instead of being present for the journey and aware of what you need to feel your best right now. You'll continue to be magnetized to disempowering thoughts, fears, and behaviors. And that will always lead to failure in the end.

Ideal Body Number

So if you don't weigh yourself, what are you supposed to use to track progress? If you don't have some kind of yardstick to compare yourself to, wouldn't you just feel like a fish out of water?

In its purest form, your future success will be determined by you consistently meeting your needs of the moment. It's only when you start living for the future that the now gets ignored. And when that happens, your behaviors are not in alignment with your needs, and inconsistency is the result.

Priority number one is being self-aware enough to know what your body needs, and that happens when you ditch the scale. It forces you into a state of self-connection, which makes identifying what you need much easier. You no longer need to solve 10 different problems – each with 10 different possible permutations, in order to arrive at your future destination. You only need to solve the problem right in front of you and the future will unfold just as it should.

THE IDEAL BODY FORMULA

Your ability to effectively meet your needs of the moment will be determined by how healed your relationships with food, body, exercise, and mind are. The more dysfunctional they are, the harder it will be for you to be aware of your needs, but also to honor them.

When your relationships are dysfunctional, you tend to be out of touch with your body. The scale and calorie counting divorce you from your own body's intuition and prevent you from trusting yourself. And the constant focus on calories and weight loss and gaining confidence through a smaller body keeps you honoring your future desires over your current needs. When that happens, neither your current needs nor your future desires are fulfilled.

So if you want to measure your progress, you measure the health of your relationships with food, body, exercise, and mind. The more healed these relationships are, the closer you are to your Ideal Body. Because that's all your Ideal Body is – the natural side effect of healed relationships. So if you want to achieve your Ideal Body, you stop measuring trivial things like calories and weight. Sure, these things might change, but they change as a side effect of you healing – not because you decide to force them to change.

You don't eat less because you say you're going to. You eat less when that happens to be the byproduct of you healing. You don't weigh less because you weigh yourself. You weigh less when that happens to be the byproduct of you healing.

To help you determine how well you are progressing in the healing process, we do away with the scale and weight as a yardstick and replace it with what we call your Ideal Body Number. This number is determined by assessing each of the four core relationships you need to heal – food, body, exercise, and mind. Through the assessment process, you are scored on a scale from 1-100. The closer to 100 you are, the more healed your relationships are and the closer you are to your Ideal Body.

The higher the number, the more confident you are; the more you trust yourself around food; the more consistent you are; the more you love moving your body; the more you feel connected to your body and identity; the more you're meeting your body's needs; the more you're accepting yourself unconditionally – all of which lead to the best possible life experience you can have. Your weight is whatever it is at that point. Depending on where you started, it could be higher, the same, or lower. But regardless of what it does, you are as happy, healthy, and as fulfilled as you could possibly be given your unique circumstances, and your life experience is amazing.

Before beginning our Built Daily Mentorship program, our new members take their initial Ideal Body Assessment. This assessment can be found right here - https://builtdaily.com/member-assessment/. Feel free to take it and see where you currently stand. Your Ideal Body Number will be calculated for you.

Whatever your starting number is, don't worry. We've seen them as low as the teens and as high as the 90s. Your only goal is to improve it by focusing on healing. As you heal, your Ideal Body gets closer and closer to becoming a reality.

Scale Tunnel Vision

Weighing yourself is not going to solve your emotional eating struggle that's being caused by you ignoring your unmet needs. It's not going to make you stop overeating on the weekends when it's the result of you being caught up in the binge/restrict cycle. It's not going to make you suddenly start liking exercise when you're forcing yourself to work out. And it's not going to help you start trusting yourself around food when you feel like eating a single cookie will turn into ten.

Why would it fix these things? How would stepping on the scale each day prevent you from coping with uncomfortable feelings using food? How is the scale going to help you feel less restricted with your eating so you stop compensating for it on the weekends? How is it going to allow you to stop seeing exercise as just a tool to burn calories? And how is it going to suddenly make you start trusting yourself around food?

The answer is – it's not. It's not going to do any of these things, yet we still rely on the scale to tell us if we're making progress. Progress towards what? Is it progress if you have a binge eating disorder yet are losing weight? Is it progress if you're still afraid to have certain foods in the house because food is controlling you? Is it progress if you lose 2 pounds but you're feeling physically and mentally horrible after eating 5,000 calories on both Saturday and Sunday and then overcompensating by eating 800 calories Monday-Friday?

For some people, that might be considered progress. If your progress is solely determined by whether or not the scale is trending down, then you might be able to make progress even if your overall life experience is suffering. But is that what you want? That's not transformation. That's body change with a side of miserable.

This is the kind of thinking the scale forces you into, though. It turns your behaviors into a sort of game that, in order to win, you only need to see the scale go down. So you ignore the real struggles and focus on rigging the system so you can see a lower number on the scale at any cost.

This is called scale tunnel vision. Everything you do is for the purpose of controlling what the scale says in the morning. You essentially start living for tomorrow's weigh-in. And when your weight isn't what you expect it to be, you double down on faulty behaviors, or you question your efforts and give up altogether.

Scale tunnel vision blinds you to the progress you're making. You start asking "what's the point?" when your weight doesn't do what you want. You know that eating well and exercising are extremely good for you, but the scale is not allowing you to think rationally – it's forcing you into an emotionally reactive state, which is difficult to navigate. At that point, the scale is like an anchor tied to your ankle while you try to swim your journey.

This is why you should focus on non-body victories (NBVs) as the better way to quantify your progress. NBVs are important for helping you break out of that scale tunnel vision, where you judge your entire journey based on what your weight is doing. They keep you from living for tomorrow's weigh-in, where every action you take is to control the number on the scale, instead of honoring what your body is needing in that moment.

Non-body victories are not the same thing as non-scale victories. When I tell people to focus on non-scale victories, they immediately start using things like tape measurements, progress pictures, or compliments from others to assess their progress. This is the body focus we're trying to get away from. It keeps you focused on outcomes. Focusing on non-body victories is what gets you back to noticing the thoughts you're thinking, the person you're being, and the things you're doing, as opposed to just what you see happening with your body. These are the things that are in your direct control.

The goal isn't weight loss. The goal is happiness, health, confidence, and an optimal life experience. Weight loss may or may not be part of that equation, but if it is, it won't be the result of you weighing yourself – it will be a side effect of you healing and addressing your underlying struggles.

Do this… picture yourself in the future when you are at your Ideal Body. Remember, your Ideal Body is the body you're in when you have healthy relationships with food, body, exercise, and mind, and are living your full life experience. It's not a what – it's a when. Now, when you are at your Ideal Body in the future, what do your thoughts and behaviors look like?

Are you emotionally eating? Are you engaging in negative self-talk when you look at yourself in the mirror? Do you trust yourself around food? Do you enjoy the physical activity you do? Do you give up at the first signs of struggle? What kind of people do you surround yourself with? Are you confident? Do you fear judgment?

These thoughts and behaviors that encompass your future ideal body are what you call your feel-best behaviors. These are the thoughts and behaviors you will be trying to incorporate into your life. They are what will be the result of you healing your relationships with food, body, exercise, and mind.

Now, the next time you get the urge to weigh yourself, ask yourself whether you feel your best? If the answer is yes, then great! Why do you need to weigh yourself then? You already feel your best. The scale can't validate that. Only you can, and you just did.

However, if you feel the urge to weigh yourself and the answer to that question is no, that you don't feel your best, then ask yourself why not. Which of your feel-best behaviors isn't being fulfilled? Are you still emotionally eating? If so, then go work on that. Weighing yourself isn't going to make you feel your best – only fixing that struggle will.

When you use the scale before you've fully healed, you run the risk of letting weight loss mask over your struggles. Only living your feel-best behaviors will make you feel your best, and the scale is not the thing that will accomplish that.

Losing Weight ≠ Being Healthy

Too many people use the terms weight loss and healthy interchangeably. But they are not synonyms.

THE IDEAL BODY FORMULA

If weight loss is going to happen, it's going to happen as a byproduct of you getting healthy. It is a side effect of improved health if the behaviors that create the improved health lead to that outcome.

Most people have this backwards. They think it's the weight loss that leads to the improved health.

But weight is a lagging indicator of behaviors. It's the behaviors that affect your health – not your weight.

If you are currently unhealthy, it's not because of your weight; it's because of your behaviors. Your weight could be completely normal in BMI terms, yet you can still be unhealthy because of your thoughts and behaviors.

This distinction between health and weight is important to understand, because too many people are using weight loss as a conduit to improved health.

When they do that, it typically results in no weight loss and no improved health. Why? Because the behaviors you engage in for losing weight are not the same as the behaviors you engage in for improving your health. Weight control behaviors rarely align with healing behaviors.

The more you focus on your weight, the harder it is to lose it. In fact, your weight loss struggle is directly proportional to the amount of time and energy you spend being focused on your weight. Weight centric approaches keep you laser-focused on the outcome and are rooted in scale and calorie-based decisions that are divorced from your body's needs.

When your body says it's hungry, you ignore it because an arbitrary calorie budget says you need to stop eating.

When your body says it needs enjoyment from exercise, you ignore it because you're more focused on workouts that burn the most fat and calories.

When your body says it wants to devour a cake, you ignore the feelings and unmet emotional needs that are driving this desire and instead double down on willpower.

These weight-loss-based decisions rarely result in improved health, because they aren't healthy behaviors. Your body doesn't care about your weight loss goals. It cares about being healthy. And it gets healthy when you consistently meet its needs. Weight loss focused behaviors tend to do the opposite and keep you stuck in the diet cycle for decades.

If you want to get healthy, then focus on getting healthy. If you want to lose weight, then focus on getting healthy. If you need to gain weight, then focus on getting healthy. Healthy people don't pursue weight-based goals – they DO healthy things.

There's no guarantee weight loss will be a side effect of improved health. That all depends on where you're starting from. But health and life experience can be improved independent of body change. In fact, many of the reasons people want to lose weight can be accomplished without ever losing a single pound.

So filter your behaviors through the lens of improved health. Do whatever is needed to heal your relationships with food, body, exercise, and mind. Be healthy while you accept whatever changes your body undergoes, as this is your unique Ideal Body.

Fear of Gaining Weight

Your fear of gaining weight is holding you back from making progress. It's keeping you stuck and preventing you from taking risks. It's keeping you from trusting yourself around food. It's keeping you from letting go of the scale and self-validating your progress. It's keeping you from choosing exercise based on what sounds enjoyable to you. And it's keeping you from accepting yourself independently of your body size.

In our heads, we've drawn a line in the sand and we fight for that weight ceiling to a fault. If you're 180lbs, nothing you do is allowed to result in you weighing 181lbs. If that happens, anxiety goes through the roof, and more times than not, you immediately stop what you're doing and return to the behaviors that had you at 180lbs. It's understandable. When someone decides they want to lose weight, the last thing they want to see happen is weight gain.

But if you only allow yourself to lose weight, you limit your ability to fix your underlying issues – the issues that are keeping you stuck in a lifetime cycle of food and body prison. You stay focused on trying to force an outcome instead of letting it happen naturally as a side effect of you healing your relationships with food, body, exercise, and mind.

Are you willing to gain 5lbs if it means you no longer obsess over calories and food? Are you willing to gain 5lbs if it means you're no longer being held emotionally hostage by the scale? Are you willing to gain 5lbs if it means you can be at peace with your body and have amazing confidence?

If you say no, you have to ask yourself why. There's some kind of meaning you've attached to that 5lbs and it's keeping you from making progress. Let's think of this differently. Are you willing to gain 5lbs in the short term if it means you achieve your ideal body in the long term?

I've worked with people who spend years and obscene amounts of time and energy stressing about a 2lb fluctuation on the scale. They convince themselves that they look drastically different and their self-worth and confidence take a hit any time they're at the top end of that 2lb range.

THE IDEAL BODY FORMULA

If this sounds like you, I'm not judging you – I'm asking you to question if that's the way you want to live your life. Because that fear is likely resulting in you doubling down on the very behaviors that are causing you so much grief in the first place.

You plan more. You try to be more perfect. You restrict more. Deprive more. Think about food more. Move more. Obsess about your body more. And do all the things that keep you from making progress. You stay stuck even though you feel in control.

Ironically, it's not even the actual weight gain that is the issue – it's the fear of weight gain. It's the fear of something that hasn't even happened.

Because the people who needed to gain weight to be at their Ideal Body have zero issue weighing more now. Why would they? They're literally at their Ideal Body now. They're happy, healthy, confident, and living their full life experience.

It's the people who fear the weight gain that struggle with their bodies the most. It's these people who never make any real progress, as they never give themselves the necessary space to heal.

That ceiling they place on their weight prevents them from being able to make eating and exercise choices that are in their best long-term interest. Instead, their healing choices have a big asterisk qualifier next to them. They think – "I'm willing to heal my relationships with food, body, exercise, and mind – *so long as* my weight only goes down". And that ends up being a recipe for failure. Because you can't create the needed space to heal when you're locked in a tiny prison.

Progress does not equal weight loss. Progress is change. Progress is transformation. Anything can happen with your weight in the short term. You might start losing weight right away. Or you could even gain some. But in the long term, you're going to gravitate to your Ideal Body and healthiest weight. And I can promise you that whatever your weight ends up being at that point, whether it's lower, the same, or higher – you won't care, because you're living your full life experience.

CHAPTER 6

REDEFINING SELF-WORTH

Your Body Is Not Your Worth

I started working out and lifting weights when I was 12 years old. The thing is, not many kids start lifting weights when they are in 5th grade. Because of this, my strength and my body stood out amongst my peers.

I got a lot of attention and compliments from both guys and girls alike. Guys wanted to know how they could build muscle and get stronger, while girls seemed to be more attracted to me.

I liked the attention – at least at the time. And I loved the compliments. But as I would soon realize, the more you live for compliments, the more you end up dying from criticism. That experience during my developmental years laid the foundation for me believing that my body was my worth. This belief eventually created debilitating insecurity, crushing social anxiety, and a full-blown binge eating disorder.

At a young age, my new identity and conditional self-worth were continually being reinforced. The supposed "good" of this situation only lasted a few years. By the time I was 16, other guys my age had started strength training for school sports, and my body no longer stood out amongst my peers. I was no longer special, so the positive reinforcement I received from my body started to diminish. And since all of my identity was tied up in my body, when I was no longer special, I lost a large part of who I was as a person.

This only got worse as the years went on. I started using food and exercise as tools to like myself more and to be more liked by others. College came, and the obsessive focus on controlling my body created a binge eating disorder. This led to out-of-control weight gain, which led to nearly 20 more years of debilitating body image struggles, Diet Culture captivity, and diminished life experience.

You might not have had the same experience as I did growing up, but make no mistake, you've also been conditioned by society that your body is your worth.

For some people, they've always been in a bigger body, and the negative attention they received reinforced the idea that their body was their worth. For others, parents, peers, coworkers, strangers, and societal messages influenced the way they valued themselves and whether they attached their worth to their body. And that has led to a lifetime of food and body obsession, weight cycling, and suboptimal life experience.

Most people are either constantly being motivated by the hope that their worth, happiness, and confidence will improve once they're in a smaller body, or they are living in fear of losing the body they have now – feeling like any weight gain will bring them a loss of self-worth and value in society.

My life started to improve once I detached my self-worth from my body and started to see the intrinsic value I had as a human being. I stopped thinking that my body was my value, and instead saw it as a vessel that added value to my life. It went from being an ornament to being an instrument. That's when everything from my binge eating disorder, to my public speaking phobia, to my overall life experience took a turn for the better.

When your self-worth and confidence are no longer determined by your weight or body, it makes it easier to eat in a way that meets your body's needs, as opposed to eating to control the way it looks (and how you feel about yourself). It makes it easier to honor your body's hunger cues. It's easier to do exercise you actually enjoy without worrying about what it will or won't do to your body. It's easier to be around people without concerning yourself with their judgments. It's easier to see your uniqueness as an asset, instead of a series of flaws. And it's easier to rediscover who you are as a person once your body is no longer defining you so strongly.

Breaking the self-worth / body bond will free you from having your life be controlled by the limiting beliefs of others – people who are as much victims of conditional self-worth as you are. So rise above this societal standard and start seeing the value you have beyond your body.

The True Meaning of Body Fat

I once asked one of our Mentorship groups what having body fat meant to them. And I got a lot of great answers.

It means I'm unattractive.

It means I don't take care of myself.

It means I have no discipline.

It means I'm not smart.

And these answers are neither right nor wrong – they're just the beliefs they're currently subscribed to.

But here's the thing… these disempowering beliefs have been conditioned into us. We've created layers and layers of meaning beyond what body fat actually is – stored calories.

THE IDEAL BODY FORMULA

Let's consider something for a moment.

A pound of fat on your body is about 3,500 calories' worth of stored energy. It is nothing more and nothing less.

Fat is just fat. It doesn't define you. It doesn't mean you're a bad person. It doesn't mean you're weak, ugly, or unworthy. And it doesn't make you less than anyone else.

It is only excess calories that have been consumed and stored for use later.

Instead, we choose, or perhaps I should say – we let, other more painful and unproductive meanings be attached to it.

We think other people will be able to see our internal struggles just by looking at us. We think that it's protecting us from potentially hurtful relationships. We think it's what's holding us back from living our full life experience.

And all of these things are in fact true simply because you've decided to let them be.

You don't have to attach any more meaning to your body fat than is necessary. You can see it for what it is – stored energy. A big butt or thighs doesn't mean you deserve any less out of life. It doesn't mean you shouldn't be loved by others, and especially not by you.

But it's hard – I get it.

Some of us are afraid to lose it, and others are afraid to have it. But it's still just body fat.

You don't have to wait to burn 3,500 calories to let go of the meaning you've attached to it. Meaning isn't stored in your fat cells – it's stored in your head.

Losing body fat doesn't release meaning from your fat cells.

The emotional pain or comfort you feel from wearing your body fat is a function of your thoughts and perspectives – not stored calories.

You can shed these thoughts without losing a single pound. You can take back the power you've given to your body fat.

But don't try to shed those thoughts by shedding weight. Thoughts don't disappear simply because you do.

Take back the power and meaning you've given to your stored energy. Shift the focus of your self-worth from your fat, back to your being. And start living your free and full life experience again.

Losing Relevancy

Many years ago, my wife and I were able to get away to Cancun without the kids. I typically struggled with my body image any time I would go on these beach vacations. And this trip was no different.

I wasn't at my leanest. I felt uncomfortable in my skin. I felt like people were watching me and judging me.

Walks to and from the ocean from our lounge chairs were uncomfortable. I was on display for all to see and judge. Ironically, I was judging myself more harshly than anyone else was judging me.

One morning, Deanna and I were sitting outside having breakfast, and I finally realized one of the reasons why I struggled so much letting go of this idea that I needed to be in a smaller, leaner body.

THE IDEAL BODY FORMULA

I felt like being in a bigger body made me less relevant in the world. I felt less relevant to my family, my friends, strangers, and especially in my business.

Interestingly, after talking through things for a while, I realized that my fears weren't unwarranted. I WAS less relevant... to some people. However, I was also becoming more relevant to others.

I was less relevant to the people who matter less and more relevant to the people who mattered more.

In other words, I became less relevant to the people who also tied their self-worth to their bodies. When they'd see me, they'd devalue me as a human being and the knowledge I shared.

This is a reflection of their own belief systems, and seeing me simply triggers those beliefs. It shines a spotlight on how they feel or might feel in a bigger body.

But to the right people – the people who see value in human beings independently of their physical appearance, I was becoming more relevant.

You get to choose the type of relevancy you want in life. But whichever one you choose, it will come with its own set of consequences.

For most of your life, you've probably chosen to tie your self-worth to your body, and because of that, you've experienced all the emotional struggles and suboptimal life experiences that come along with that choice.

The choice may not have been done on purpose. You were probably like most people, stuck as an unknowing victim of Diet Culture. But you experienced the consequences nonetheless.

However, you can choose to be relevant and valued and worthy right now. I don't mean tomorrow or after you lose a few pounds. I mean right now as you sit there reading this book.

It is a choice. And it happens in an instant. Because self-worth and relevancy are a function of the mind – not the body.

And if you choose wisely, you will attract the people who see you, the person – not you, the body. Your relationships will get deeper and you will have a fuller life experience.

Your relevancy to the people you don't want in your life will diminish, but it will grow with the people you truly want to be surrounded by. In fact, those other people won't even matter to you anymore. Because when you start seeing your worth, you'll stop seeing those who don't.

Conditional Confidence

How many times have you heard the message that you should lose weight so that you can be more confident?

This idea that weight loss leads to improved confidence is yet another reason we believe that our body is our worth.

And if I'm being honest, I used to believe that losing weight made people more confident too. In fact, I'd get annoyed any time someone tried to tell me otherwise.

This was always something that didn't sit right with me. Even well after I had ditched Diet Culture and was coaching people through the Ideal Body Formula, I still struggled with this idea that losing weight didn't make you more confident.

After all, I had been leaner in my life many times. And each and every time my confidence improved.

And I know that you have probably lost 5, 10, or 20+ pounds in your life at one point and experienced an improved level of self-confidence and self-worth. So how can I sit here and tell you that losing weight doesn't make you more confident?

Here's the thing, it DOES make you more confident. But it's not real confidence – it's what we call conditional confidence.

Conditional confidence ties your confidence and self-worth to your body. It reinforces the idea that your body is your worth.

Why does this matter? Because most people spend their entire life playing in the Diet Culture sandbox, gaining and losing weight, and never stepping into their true confidence.

They go through waves of confidence that are 100% conditional on them losing weight. So when they aren't in a smaller body, they value themselves less, and they lack self-confidence.

If you want to be more confident, then be more confident. Stop tying this confidence to some body or some thing.

Conditional confidence is fragile. It's always a few pounds gained away from being taken away from you.

True confidence comes from within – from the self. It's not created from external things or given to you by other people. That's why it's called self-confidence and not others-confidence.

What you're after is unconditional confidence – confidence that operates independently of your body, circumstances, possessions, or other value-seeking things.

True unconditional confidence comes from unconditional acceptance of your self and your body. You need to start giving yourself permission to be confident right now instead of pretending like you have to earn it through body manipulation.

Unconditional confidence isn't earned – it's taken. Better yet, it's found, as you've always had it. It's just been wallpapered over by a lifetime of limiting beliefs. It's the rejection of all these limiting beliefs you have of yourself, and the unconditional acceptance of who you are as a human being that brings that confidence back to the surface. It doesn't come from changing your body – it comes from accepting your self. It's not about what you see in the mirror – it's about who you see looking back.

When you see someone who is truly confident, it's because they own who they are and what they look like. This is a choice you make. Nothing about your outside world needs to change for you to be more confident. It's only your inside world that needs connecting with.

Seeking Validation

It's been years since I've posted a shirtless pic of myself on social media, and I don't plan to ever go back.

Since I made the decision to stop, not only has my body image dramatically improved, but so has my business and the types of people I attract to it.

It wasn't easy to stop. Any time I posted a shirtless pic, the engagement on my posts were at times 10x more than when I didn't.

Not only that, but people would suddenly start messaging me, asking me about what programs I had available and inquiring about coaching.

The compliments and attention felt good, but they also blinded me to the consequences.

I was keeping myself stuck in a perpetual cycle of tying my body to my worth.

THE IDEAL BODY FORMULA

Post shirtless pic. Get lots of attention. Feel more worthy. Repeat.

Don't post shirtless pic. Get less attention. Feel less worthy. Repeat. Or rather, go back to posting a shirtless pic.

And worse, those shirtless pics ended up repelling my ideal clients and attracting more of Diet Culture.

Don't get me wrong, I don't want to body shame anyone. There's nothing inherently wrong with showing your body or being proud of it. Or, in my case, helping people see and believe that healing your relationships with food, body, exercise, and mind absolutely will result in you achieving your healthiest weight.

But there's a time, a place, and a purpose to do it. And I, like most people, was using it to validate myself, instead of to help others.

There's a very important lesson you can learn from my experience…

So long as you try to feel more valuable by changing your body, you will continue to attract people who only value you for your body.

You attract the values you project.

If you think your body is your worth, then those are the people who will be attracted to you.

To me, it's better to be liked and valued unconditionally by 1000 people than to have conditional admiration by millions. I'd rather be rejected at my new standard than be accepted at my old one.

Giving up these self-serving shirtless pics has helped me to find value elsewhere and has made it 10x easier to eat and move my body in a way that makes me happy, instead of basing every decision on what it would do to my body (aka my worth).

And it has helped me to create a business and a community of like-minded individuals with whom I have deeper connections. Because what really truly adds value to yours and other people's lives is you living as your authentic self, as that is what's going to give people the courage to be themselves too.

When you ditch Diet Culture and the idea that your body is your worth, you aren't giving up on yourself – you're going all in on yourself. And you allow others to go all in on you (and themselves) too.

Diversifying Your Self-Worth

Most people have the majority of their self-worth tied up in their body. It's really easy for this to happen. The beauty industry spends many billions of dollars a year helping you tie your worth to your body.

That makes it easy to pick a perfectly natural body feature and make a problem out of it. Greying hair? Let's make that a problem. Wrinkles? Sure… that's a problem. Cellulite? Why not make that a problem too.

And of course, we have our weight. A perfectly normal body nowadays might not conform to societal beauty standards. So everyone spends their time, money, and energy chasing after an ideal they believe will give them more standing in society.

Our body isn't the only thing we tie our worth to, though. It just happens to be one of, if not the biggest thing. We also derive self-worth from our net worth, our career, our achievements, our possessions, and our intelligence, to name a few.

But you'll notice something with all of these "worth enhancers" – they are all externally derived. We seek out our self-worth in external things. And while it's not necessarily wrong to derive some worth from these things, the problem is that you feel like you have to earn your worth. The assumption is that you don't have value unless you make an effort, achieve something, and earn it.

This is social conditioning at its finest. Think about it. When a baby is born, does it have value? Of course it does. All human beings have an inherent self-worth that is more valuable than all the other external things combined.

You came into this world a whole human being. And slowly but surely, that wholeness has been stripped away from you.

A lifetime of experiences has created limiting beliefs that have cast doubt on ourselves, diminished our self-worth, and led us to believe we have to earn the right to feel whole again.

What most of us don't realize is all we're really trying to do in life is get back to that state of wholeness where our true life experience begins.

So the solution isn't really to pursue goals of excellence – it's to let go of the baggage that is keeping us from living as our whole selves where unlimited potential exists.

Your job is to turn inwards and start diversifying your self-worth away from your body and external things, and reconnect with your inherent self-worth and values. This shift in derived self-worth is what's going to enable you to see yourself as a whole and valuable human being so that not only will you start eating and moving your body from a place of self-love and acceptance, but you will start to experience your entire life differently.

Before, your self-worth looked like a pie chart. Your body made up the biggest slice, and then the other slices were mostly other externally derived things such as wealth, achievements, etc.

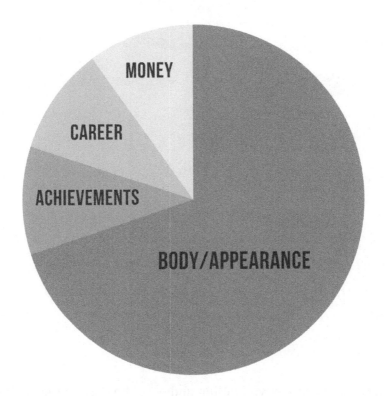

But going forward, your self-worth will be represented by a hub and spoke model. Picture a bike wheel with a center hub and a bunch of spokes coming out from it. In the center, you have the most important part of your self-worth – your inherent self-worth. And then each spoke from that hub represents a value that's important to you – a value that you choose to live through. These values might be things like honesty, kindness, integrity, authenticity, compassion, empathy, creativity, growth, humor, optimism, or respect.

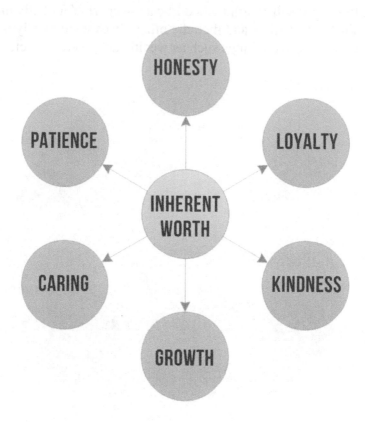

These aren't things you go out and get. They aren't things that you achieve. They are what you *be*. They are your identity. And they are what will add value to your life.

The desirable outcomes that happen in your life are a byproduct of this self-worth model. They are natural side effects of identity. With the pie chart model of self-worth, people look to cultivate a certain identity by changing their external situation, and then by relying on the social conditioning of others to accept their new status.

Remember, self-worth is derived from the self. The value you have as a human being comes from within. No amount of social conditioning can take that away.

CHAPTER 7

NEGATIVE SELF-TALK

You're Fat

Many years ago, I approached a guy who was about my height. He had his shirt off and was getting ready to go swimming.

Personally, I thought the guy looked absolutely ridiculous. He was pale, had the worst spare tire, and his muscle tone was nowhere to be found.

I couldn't help myself. The words that came out of my mouth were automatic.

I said, "Wow, you're fat! How can you not be embarrassed going to the pool looking like that? Go to the gym. Stay away from the Twinkies. A tan wouldn't hurt you either!"

The guy looked me straight in the eyes, a defeated look on his face, sighed, and then didn't say another word. He put his shirt back on and went about his day.

I felt pretty bad saying those things, but I really didn't feel much remorse. I had looked at that same guy in the mirror every day for years, picking apart my body.

THE IDEAL BODY FORMULA

Obviously, I was talking to myself here, as I would never say these things to another person. But that's the problem. We will defend other people from blatant criticism and verbal abuse with passion, but when it comes to the things we say to ourselves, we just write it off and accept it.

And make no mistake, negative self-talk is verbal abuse. Verbal abuse is using words to manipulate, intimidate, and maintain power and control over someone (or yourself, in this case). It's disrespectful, harmful, disempowering, and it diminishes your life experience. This is exactly what negative self-talk is and does.

If you wouldn't walk up to a random person, let alone a person you're supposed to love, and tell them to their face that they're fat, ugly, worthless, and should be ashamed of their body, then why would you do that to yourself? It's time you start treating yourself the way you want others to be treated.

When my wife, Deanna, did her yearly retreat with moms, one of the activities she had them do was to write down a handful of negative things they say to themselves when they look in the mirror. This is quite an enlightening experience in and of itself. Actually seeing these comments written down is eye-opening.

But she takes it a step further. She then has each person turn to the person next to them and say the things they've written down. Half the people can't bring themselves to say these things to another person. And the other half break down and start crying.

It's tough, but it shows one very important thing – we don't pay ourselves the same kindness and respect as we do to others. We don't have the same standards. And we've become desensitized to all the ways we put ourselves down.

You might think that guilting and shaming yourself and your body will motivate you to take action, but I can assure you that the actions you take won't be the right behaviors you need to make.

Behaviors that are born from a place of self-hate, disrespect, and disgust are much different than the behaviors spurred from a place of self-love, respect, and self-care. The way you treat yourself matters. The words you use to describe yourself matter.

This whole "hating yourself into changing your body" thing never works. It negatively influences the way you approach your eating and exercise. You end up eating to control your body instead of to respect and give it what it needs to thrive. You end up exercising to burn calories and purge fat instead of to enjoy and celebrate movement. We take care of the things we value, and we neglect the things that we hate.

We're all so worried about the people around us and the toxic relationships that make us miserable, yet we don't even realize that the most toxic relationship most people have is with themselves. We will live with ourselves 24/7 for the rest of our lives, yet we allow this toxicity to be part of our life, and it affects everything from our self-worth, to our confidence, to the life experiences we miss out on because we feel less-than.

It's time for you to get mad – mad at the person inside of you who is constantly attacking your being. Defend yourself the same way you'd defend your kid or your partner if someone walked up to them and told them they were fat, ugly, or should be ashamed of being themselves in this world.

The confidence you're seeking through body manipulation doesn't come from changing your body – it comes from standing up for yourself. It comes from respecting your body and what it looks like. It comes from acceptance and self-compassion.

So the next time you get a glimpse of yourself in the mirror and start down the road of negative self-talk, say NO and tell that person, that toxic ego, to get lost. They are no longer welcome to share the same place in your head as the person you're trying to become. You're no longer going to accept anything less than respect from yourself. Because you deserve to be treated as the valued human being you are.

Separate Yourself From Your Thoughts

You are not your thoughts. I know it might feel that way sometimes, as they absolutely affect your life experience. But they are not YOU.

You are the one who observes your thoughts. You are your self. Your thoughts, on the other hand, form your ego.

For a lot of people, their thoughts and ego overtake their self. They have a hard time dissociating from the inner dialogue that's running through their head. So when that dialogue is full of negative self-talk, it gets internalized as truth and negatively affects your body image and overall life experience.

Your thoughts are created by a process that's based on your prior life experiences, which create your belief system, which then filters your current reality. Because of this, your thoughts feel very real to you. However, they are just a construct of your past.

Think of it this way – when you were born, you were almost entirely your SELF. You had an existence without much thought, as there had been few, if any, experiences to create a belief system. But as time went on, you began to receive inputs from your environment. You saw things, heard things, and felt things. You had experiences.

You started to be conditioned by your parents and society. You were taught what was good or bad; what was shameful or prideful; when you should feel guilty or happy; what a healthy or attractive body looked like; what made you valuable. And your belief system was formed.

NEGATIVE SELF-TALK

Your belief system is like your operating system. It inputs stimuli from your environment – things you see, for example, and outputs thoughts and behaviors. When you've been conditioned to believe that a certain-sized body is unattractive, then when you look in the mirror and see an image that doesn't match the societal ideal, you experience negative self-talk.

Ironically, this negative self-talk is there to protect you. It's just doing it in an ineffective way that's based on false premises. Your ego is trying to protect itself from being hurt. It doesn't want to be called fat or ugly. That would be painful. So you develop an inner critic to help keep you safe. The idea is that this negative self-talk will either create a preemptive shield to criticism from others in the future or it will spur you into action and do something about your body so that you don't experience pain.

But remember, you are not your thoughts. This entire reality that you've created is simply your past experiences and traumas being dragged to the now. Your true self is the one who is observing these thoughts and is the one who has the power to neutralize them.

Because you really aren't in danger. Any danger you are experiencing with your body is self-imposed. The threat was created to protect your ego from emotional discomfort – not your body from physical pain.

In reality, your negative self-talk is the real threat. It is limiting your ability to believe in yourself and your own ability to reach your potential. These thoughts are limiting your ability to make positive changes in your life. They lower your ability to see and capitalize on opportunities for personal growth.

So your goal is to separate yourself from your thoughts by understanding that you are not your thoughts. Observe your thoughts. Understand where they are coming from. Understand that they are simply trying to keep you safe from danger. But then realize the threat you are defending against isn't real. You aren't actually in danger. The danger is a manifestation of your past experiences being brought to the present moment.

You don't have to continue internalizing your thoughts. You can pick and choose the ones you want to be part of your identity. When your negative self-talk doesn't align with who you want to be or how you want to feel, say thanks but no thanks. Observe the thought and let it pass through you. Don't latch onto it and become it.

The more you create this distance between yourself and your thoughts, the better you'll be able to harness your inner critic for good. You'll be able to let go of your experiences of the past that cloud your empowering belief system, and you'll be able to start directing your future by being more selective with the thoughts you internalize.

Reacting to Your Inner Critic

Your inner critic is there to help you recognize when you're acting out of alignment with your belief system. When things get out of alignment, that's when negative self-talk commences.

It's normal to have an inner critic, and it's normal to have negative self-talk. Pretending these perfectly normal things don't exist isn't going to help you manage them when you inevitably experience them.

The problem isn't that we experience negative self-talk; it's that we act reactively to it. When this happens, we tend to act irrationally, engaging in diet-like behaviors, which throws us into a downward spiral.

So how do we know when our inner critic is at work? Feeling guilt and shame are a couple of signs to be on the lookout for. But they aren't the only signs. It's also normal to catastrophize (worst-case scenario thinking), personalize (believing everything is your fault), filter (only seeing the bad), or have feelings of doubt or worthlessness. All of these things happen when you experience something that's out of alignment with your belief system.

So we need to approach our inner critic and negative self-talk from two fronts – proactively and reactively. Proactively, we need to challenge our beliefs that are leading to unwarranted self-talk. But we also need to react to our inner critic in a productive way. It's not about "being positive" either, or taking the negative self-talk and trying to force it into positive self-talk. That isn't always going to be possible, reasonable, or even productive, and can be a form of toxic positivity. It's more about neutralizing the negative by investigating and challenging your limiting beliefs.

If you're feeling shame around your body, or you're experiencing guilt or beating yourself up for overeating, then there's an underlying belief that is triggering your inner critic. The negative self-talk is there to show you that you did or are doing something wrong (true or not), so that you can do something about it.

The belief might be that your body should be smaller or that you should weigh less. So any appearance to the contrary, or any behavior with your eating that might lead you away from that belief, is going to trigger your inner critic. And for most people in this scenario, they are going to react emotionally by restricting calories, depriving themselves of certain foods, and doubling down on willpower – the Diet Culture approach that fails 99% of the time.

Now, while it's natural to feel guilt and shame, not every scenario justifies them raising their voices. If you go and inflict physical harm on someone, you might very well feel guilt and shame, and it will probably be warranted. However, if you feel guilt and shame because your body looks a certain way, then this is when you want to be proactive and challenge the underlying beliefs that are leading to you feeling this way. We'll talk about how to do this more in Chapter 14.

While you're working on being proactive with your negative self-talk, you're still very likely to experience these feelings. And while it's normal to feel this way, we don't want to act from this place.

Beating yourself up and guilting and shaming yourself is a form of self-punishment. Unfortunately, when you punish yourself for doing something wrong, it doesn't teach you how to do it right. Instead, you end up reacting emotionally using avoidance behaviors (with dieting being the big one).

What you want to do is validate your inner critic, as it is useful for recognizing when you're acting out of alignment. But once you experience those feelings, you don't want to emotionally react to them. That just results in compensatory behaviors that treat surface-level symptoms (i.e., dieting). Instead, you want to investigate the situation so that you can act rationally to address the actual problem (if there even is one).

Remember, it's not about denying your inner critic or fighting against negative self-talk. It's about understanding where it's coming from so that you can potentially address the limiting beliefs that are driving it, and then learning to react to it in a way that will actually be productive.

#Don't Hate – Investigate

Beating yourself up for doing something wrong doesn't accomplish anything. It might feel like it does because it's a form of self-inflicted punishment. In a way, it helps us excuse our behavior.

But we don't need to hate on ourselves when we do something wrong. We don't need to beat ourselves up for overeating on the weekend. We don't need to trash talk our bodies when we look in the mirror.

Doing so isn't going to lead to the behaviors you need to feel better. Instead, the negative self-talk leads to punitive behaviors like dieting. Reactions tend to be extreme and emotional, which rarely align with your body's needs.

When you overeat on the weekend, you question what's wrong with yourself and guilt yourself into lecturing that you should be able to do better. You end up associating your worth as a human being with your ability to adhere to a behavior. Never mind that the behavior was a byproduct of Diet Culture and set you up for failure in the first place. So your solution is to double down on willpower and discipline, bust out the "no excuses" philosophy, make your diet even more perfect, lower your calories, and work just a little harder by burning extra calories in the gym.

And we all know how that goes. But what we don't realize is how this extreme behavior is the side effect of negative self-talk. Negative self-talk doesn't have to mean you're literally talking out loud to yourself in a bully-like way, although that certainly can happen. It also means the running dialogue of thought that happens both consciously and unconsciously that directs our behaviors.

This is the sneaky self-talk. It happens on auto-pilot and keeps you stuck in a cycle of self-hate and suboptimal behaviors. And when it comes to your health and fitness journey, the negative self-talk can almost always be traced back to your body directly, or indirectly, by how your behaviors are affecting it.

The solution? #DontHateInvestigate. Deanna would kill me if I didn't give her credit for this little phrase. It's her mantra, and it's a great one to live by.

"Don't hate – investigate" means to raise your self-awareness out of the stream of unconscious negative self-talk so that you can productively assess and deal with a situation. We're all going to mess up. No one is going to achieve their Ideal Body without any hiccups along the way. It's what you do during these inflection points that determines whether you keep moving forward or if you get dragged back into Diet Culture.

When you overeat on the weekend, you might be currently conditioned to start running your negative self-talk programming. And like I said earlier, this leads to knee-jerk emotional behaviors (overcompensating by eating less or purging those calories by moving more) that have very little chance of helping you succeed. However, when you "don't hate – investigate," it allows you to dissect the situation from outside of the emotional cloud so that you can investigate it and address the root cause of the unwanted behavior.

Overeating on the weekend could have been caused by emotional eating, or it could've been a byproduct of too much restriction and deprivation during the week that created a spring-like effect come the weekend. If you let negative self-talk run your future, you'll never be able to see these causes, and you'll instead focus on the outcome and what actually happened, try to treat the symptom, and strong-arm it into submission by implementing behaviors that don't address the underlying causes. You end up being a symptom treater, and the problem behavior will persist.

"Don't hate – investigate" means you rationally investigate the situation to find the root cause. And then you address that directly. That's the entire essence of the Ideal Body Formula. You achieve your Ideal Body by healing your relationships with food, body, exercise, and mind, which happens by addressing your struggles at their origin.

So when you find yourself engaging with your negative self-talk, understand that while it might feel like you deserve it or that it's pushing you to take action, it's not getting you to take the type of action that will prevent it from happening again. It's actually priming you to remain stuck in the cycle, and if you aren't careful, you will spend a lifetime in the diet cycle. Instead, "don't hate – investigate".

Fat Tony!

Before I started my fitness business back in 2011, I spent 5 years in Afghanistan working for the military, managing their communications network.

While living on the base, I did my best to stay in shape. I worked out in the gym and ate the food they provided in their chow halls.

It wasn't perfect, but I got done with what I needed to. However, my binge eating disorder followed me to the other side of the world.

On one of the bases, there was a small Tim Hortons. For those who don't know what this place is, it's very similar to a Krispy Kreme restaurant.

Several times per week, I'd go and get a dozen donuts or a few dozen donut holes, shamelessly walk them back to my living quarters, and eat them all.

My bingeing was in full swing, and my body was affected.

In fact, one of my co-workers saw my body in the shower area and found it cute to start calling me "Fat Tony".

For a week after that encounter, that's what he referred to me as. He would even yell it from a distance to get my attention – "Fat Tony!"

THE IDEAL BODY FORMULA

That was until I confronted him on it and told him to knock it off. He laughed about it and said he was just kidding, but I told him to start making jokes at his own expense.

He never did it again.

I tell you this story because me standing up for myself was a form of body/self-respect. And that's something a lot of people are lacking.

We mentally, verbally, and physically assault our bodies and allow others to cross boundaries we don't defend.

It's time to start standing up for yourself. No one is going to respect you until you respect yourself first.

No one is going to fully love and accept you until you fully love and accept yourself first.

No one is going to validate your self-worth until you validate it first.

How can you expect other people to treat you with respect and body kindness if you can't even do it for yourself? We show other people how to treat us by the way we treat ourselves.

You don't become beautiful by believing you're ugly. You don't become smart by thinking you're dumb. And you don't love and accept your body by hating and rejecting it. Hating your body doesn't make you like it more. It doesn't matter what behaviors you insert along the way.

So start having some compassion for yourself. Stand up for yourself. Stop beating yourself up for the mistakes of your past. And start embracing who you are and what you look like.

You don't have to hate your body to be motivated to change it. There is another way – a way that's born out of self-respect.

CHAPTER 8

HANDLING JUDGMENT

Hiding Behind a Pen Name

I had just come off a 5-year work contract in Afghanistan working for the Army. This was my first real job that required me to step up and be a leader.

And it stressed me out. Interestingly enough, it wasn't the nightly mortar attacks on the base or the occasional car bombs at the front gates that stressed me out – it was the constant leadership meetings and the threat of me having to share my thoughts.

That might sound silly, but I held onto a lot of fear of judgment in my life. It affected every single part of it, from work, to my social life, to simply going out into public.

When I returned to the states, I was determined to find a way to not have to deal with that environment anymore. So I tried my hand at blogging. I was passionate about fitness, and I liked to write, so it seemed like a perfect fit.

So, I started my first blog and business, Coach Calorie, back in 2011, and I sat at home using my written words to convey my value to others. In fact, I never even showed myself. Coach

THE IDEAL BODY FORMULA

Calorie was my pen name. I was too afraid to put myself out there for the public to see and judge.

In my head, I worried that if people saw what I looked like, it wouldn't line up with the knowledge that I shared. I was fit, but I thought I needed to have a certain look to be taken seriously. And if I didn't have the body to match the words, then I would lose credibility.

The blog grew fast... extremely fast. I gained over 100,000 followers on Facebook in just a few months. Companies, magazines, and podcasters started reaching out to me to interview me. But I would just say no, or even ignore their requests, because it stressed me out to even think about it. What if I messed up? What if I didn't have the right answer? What would they think of me then?

The fear of judgment was crippling. I started this business to avoid the fear of public speaking and judgment, and here I was feeling under threat even more than before.

The longer I went without showing what I looked like, the bigger the fear grew. Until one day, I decided enough was enough. I did a big reveal and posted a small picture of myself – a 2in x 2in avatar. And the responses were surprising.

First of all, no one said anything negative. No one criticized my appearance. No one suddenly didn't take my writing seriously.

Someone did think I was a woman this whole time. Others said I was attractive. But most people just went on with their own lives and didn't think twice about it.

And that's the thing with judgment. We are so worried about everyone else judging us that we don't realize the most crippling part of it is our own self-judgment.

HANDLING JUDGMENT

We get so self-absorbed that we think the entire world is revolving around us and what we think, say, do, or look like. We over-value other people's opinions. We try to get our bodies to look a certain way so that we can be judged favorably, when in reality, no one really cares. The degree of our self-importance gets way out of alignment with the reality of how much other people really care.

We start living a life of what ifs. What if they think this about me? What if they think I'm fat, stupid, clumsy, weak, or old?

Well... what if they do? Why does it matter so much what other people think of you? The bigger question is, what do you think of yourself? Because your self-judgment has a much bigger impact on your life.

Avoiding Discomfort

The real problem with fearing judgment of your body isn't the feeling of emotional discomfort you do experience – it's the parts of your life you don't experience.

Whether judgment is coming from other people or if it's your own self-judgment, we tend to focus on avoiding the emotional discomfort associated with it at all costs. It's one of the reasons we go through such great lengths to change our bodies.

But the true cost of fearing judgment is how small your life becomes. You become hyper-focused on curating your life in a way that accounts for all potential threats of judgment and criticism.

You end up living in a box, a very small comfort zone, which prevents you from taking risks in your life. You avoid seeing people, going places, doing things, and being the person you truly want to be.

You don't pursue things in your career, you don't take the vacations you want to take, you miss out on intimacy with your partner, you avoid going back to school, and you close yourself off to any other opportunity that might put you face to face with judgment.

The thing with judgment is that it's never going away. It's as natural as eating. We all do it, and we always will. So, you have to stop trying to avoid it and start working with it.

You might think you're avoiding it by closing yourself off to other people, but all that's happening is your own self-judgment is putting you into a protective bubble. You feel safe, but only because you have a few inches of safety between you and the real world. In reality, you aren't winning the war against judgment; judgment has you in a checkmate scenario – backed into a corner, unable to experience life.

What people don't understand is that we don't do all this work of handling judgment so that we can go into a situation comfortable. We do the work so that we can go into the situation despite the discomfort.

Because, as I said, the real threat isn't the discomfort – it's the loss of life experience. We need to work through the judgment so that we can live life.

It's not the lack of discomfort that allows you to live your life to the fullest; it's having life experiences in the face of discomfort that allows you to get more comfortable with the judgment.

Understanding the judgment, knowing where it's coming from, and putting it into perspective are all part of the process for getting you to step outside of your comfort zone so that you can have some new experiences – experiences that provide you with new evidence that you are safe and capable of being yourself in this world.

So, be careful that you don't fall into the trap of doing so much personal development work trying to wipe judgment from your existence. It's not going to happen. Instead, do just enough that allows you to take action in the face of discomfort, as new empowering experiences are what allow you to overcome judgment's grip on your life.

Getting Offended

One thing is for certain – at some point on your Ideal Body journey, someone is going to say something, and you're going to get offended.

They may say something directly to you, or you may read or hear the words of another person being directed to someone else. Either way, their opinions, also known as their judgments and beliefs, are bound to cause you some discomfort eventually.

The important thing to understand here is where the responsibility lies for you feeling better. Because while someone judging you is their problem, you getting offended by their judgment is yours.

If you don't want either direct or indirect judgment to bother you, you have to understand why it's causing you discomfort in the first place.

Getting offended is a sign that somebody is either challenging one of your beliefs, or they are affirming a belief of yours that causes you discomfort. Regardless, it's your responsibility to either release the ownership of someone else's judgment or to explore your own self-judgment that others are simply confirming.

The first thing you want to do when you start feeling offended is to ask yourself, "why is this bothering me?"

What you're trying to determine here is if you getting offended is a result of one of your underlying beliefs either getting challenged or affirmed.

If it's getting challenged, then you can decide whether you want to hold onto your current belief or adopt the belief/judgment of the other person. If you don't like what they think, then you don't have to take ownership of it.

You don't need to fight for your own belief. You just need to let them own theirs. They created their belief through a lifetime of experiences. It is not your responsibility to get them to change their beliefs. So just say "no, thank you" and move on.

If, on the other hand, you get offended because they are affirming an underlying belief of yours that causes you pain, it is still your responsibility to feel better. They are simply telling you what you already know. So how can you really get offended at that?

If someone calls you fat or says you have cellulite, you have to ask why this is even a problem. Why does this bother you more than them saying you have 2 hands?

It's because you have attached disempowering meaning to these things. So this is your problem to solve. Your emotions are a result of your own thoughts and beliefs – not the actions of others. It would be nice if the situation never happened. But it did. If you want to feel better, the solution comes from within you.

If someone were to call you a mailbox, you would just laugh it off. The only reason you're offended is because on some level you believe what people say is true. So all that's happening is you're getting upset at yourself.

What people call having "thick skin" is simply metaphorical armor resulting from the correct allocation of belief ownership.

They either reflect the judgment back to the other person by not taking ownership of it, or they take responsibility for their own beliefs.

With the latter, there is no real feeling offended, as feeling offended is the result of denial, not acceptance. When you take ownership of your beliefs, confirmation via someone's judgment doesn't have an effect on you. Why would it? You already know. It's the denial of your own beliefs that causes you to feel offended. Much of our fear of other people's opinions simply comes from a lack of conviction and acceptance in who we believe we are.

In the end, all judgment is self-judgment. It doesn't matter where it's coming from. It's always a projection of somebody's underlying belief system. So decide where the ownership lies and decide whose responsibility it is to work on changing the beliefs or accepting them.

Building Your Armor

Most of us handle judgment in a very inefficient way. We attempt to address each instance of judgment individually.

When someone judges you, you address that particular judgment and the individual criticizing you. This seems like a reasonable thing to do, but the approach starts to break down once you try to scale the strategy.

My business requires me to share my philosophy. I do this in many ways – articles, videos, a book, etc. When I put myself and my thoughts out into the world, I open myself up to judgment and criticism. And the more my ideas resonate with people, the bigger my audience grows, and the more judgment I have to handle.

When I first started writing and sharing images of myself, the majority of people were kind. They loved what I shared, as it helped them overcome their own struggles. But that didn't mean there weren't people who disagreed with me. And some of those people didn't care to share their opinions of my work in a respectful way.

Sometimes they'd criticize my work itself. They'd say it was dumb or wrong. But other times they'd make it personal. They'd tell me I was dumb. I was an idiot. They'd call me a clown. They'd say that because I didn't have a string of letters after my name that I had no business coaching people. They'd even body shame me, call me ugly, or tell me they wish I'd die.

Back then, I'd address each judgment and criticism at its source. If someone left a comment on social media, I would react and write something back defending myself. If someone sent me an email shaming my appearance, I'd reply and say something back.

Sometimes I wouldn't directly reply to the criticism. But behind the scenes, I was molding myself into someone that would avoid judgment. As a result, I would try to anticipate the criticism and avoid being hurt by not putting my authentic self and thoughts forward.

This is how most people operate their lives. Everything they do when they step out of the house or come out of their safe space is influenced by what others are thinking about them. The clothes you wear, the words you use, the way you walk, the car you drive – everything you do has this conformity angle to it that is based in judgment avoidance. And when the random criticism comes up, you address it directly.

I quickly realized this wasn't going to work for me. As my audience doubled and then doubled many more times, so did the actual judgments. It felt like I was drowning. It got to the point that my audience grew big enough that every day someone was criticizing me. I'd wake up to negative comments. I'd go to bed seeing them. And it really crushed me.

Keep in mind that this was probably less than 1% of the overall comments I received. The other 99 out of 100 were amazing comments from amazing people. But that's not how us humans experience things. If someone compliments you 100 times, and then makes fun of you once, you remember that one time – sometimes for the rest of your life.

Picture yourself facing a line of 10 people all facing you. Draw a line from each person directly to you. This line is their judgment and criticism. Put a shield up on each of those 10 lines. This is you addressing those criticisms. You have one shield per person per criticism. If there were 100 people, there would be 100 lines (judgments) to you and 100 shields of you addressing them. It looks like this...

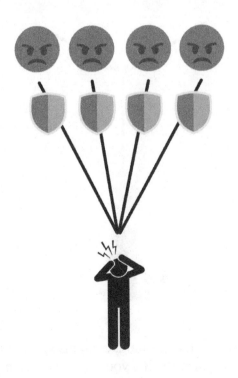

This is how most people handle judgment. And you can see how it might be easy with 1 or 2 people, but as your world grows, it becomes too much to handle. And keep in mind that this doesn't include all the imaginary judgments you handle, aka the judgments you think people are making but were never verbalized. These tend to outnumber the real judgments by a factor of 100 to 1 or more.

Now imagine that same row of 10 people. Draw a line from each of those people to one singular point right in front of you. Put your one single shield right there. All the lines (judgments) converge to this singular point before they make it to you. If there are 100 or 1000 people, then they all still converge to this one point.

This one single point, this shield, contains all your beliefs about yourself. It's your identity. It's your love and acceptance of your true self. It's your self-worth. And it's your trust and confidence in who you are.

This is your armor. It repels judgment and criticism. It doesn't allow it past the shield. It doesn't get internalized. And it doesn't influence who you are or force you to mold yourself to others' opinions.

This is how you should handle judgment – from a singular point. You don't have to manage the beliefs and identities of others. They just get deflected off your shield, because you're confident in who you are and you understand that their judgments have nothing to do with you.

As my audience grew, I adopted this new mindset. I was able to handle more and more criticism and judgment. I stopped replying to the haters. I stopped internalizing what they said. Criticism that used to take me a week or more to get over, now never even made it into me. I'd read it and move on. In fact, I started to have more compassion for others, because I understood their judgment was a reflection of a crippling belief system they were living by.

You don't need a large audience of fans to start implementing this concept. Remember, the imaginary judgment is the bigger threat anyways. Every day you put yourself out into the world, and if you don't take unconditional ownership of yourself, you're going to let the opinions of others take ownership of you.

The Mirror of Judgment

What do you notice in the world? What do you notice about other people? What are the personality traits that stand out to you in others? What parts of their appearance do you tend to notice?

When you watch TV, do you find yourself wondering how old someone is? Who their spouse is? How much they weigh or what their workout program is? How much money they make? When you notice people in public, do you see cellulite on them? Their wrinkles? Or the kind of clothes they wear?

You might not realize it, but all throughout your day, you are making snap judgments about things in your environment. Sometimes these are micro judgments (i.e., noticing things) that happen subconsciously, and other times they are full-blown conscious judgments of others.

Regardless, these judgments are the window into what matters to you. That's the thing about judging people – it's never about the other person. It's always about you and your underlying beliefs and value system.

If you are always noticing aging characteristics of people in public, or you are always wondering how old someone is on TV, it's because you personally value something about aging. And that value influences the way you go about your life and where you place your emotional energy.

If you tend to notice the size of people's bodies, their physiques, their cellulite, or other qualities, then it's because you value being a certain size or looking a certain way. The belief system that filters your world to notice these things will have an effect on your own behaviors and life experience.

None of this is good or bad, by the way. Remember… judgment is normal. The important thing to understand is why this is happening.

Other people are simply mirrors. They are mirroring your own personal belief system back to you. The judgments you have are not about others – they are about you. You noticed something in someone that was aligned/misaligned with your belief system.

Think about it. Do you think your judgment of that person is the same judgment that 100 other people will have? Of course not.

Each person will believe something different about that same person. The person never changed, though. They are the constant. What changed were the judgments of the person. And that's because each person has their own unique belief and value system.

Each person is getting their own judgments mirrored back to them. These judgments are the culmination of a lifetime of experiences and social conditioning.

This mirror of judgment is important for two reasons. One, it helps you overcome judgment from others, as it helps you to depersonalize it. If you know receiving judgment and criticism isn't about you, but rather about others, then it makes it so much easier not to internalize it and affect your quality of life. And two, if you can be self-aware enough to understand that your own judgments are a reflection of you and what you value, you can change the limiting beliefs that are impacting your life.

You can stop yourself when you find you're being critical of others, and you can question where that belief is coming from and whether it's a belief you want to continue subscribing to. You can ask yourself whether that belief is making you happier or if it's taking away from your life experience.

What you'll find is that as you challenge your own beliefs and change them, you start experiencing your environment differently. You start noticing different things because you now value different things. You see people differently because you see yourself differently. You start seeing people as whole human beings instead of the sum of their body parts.

How Others See You

There is no absolute truth to who you are in other people's eyes. Everyone is going to see you differently, and their perspective is the culmination of a lifetime of conditioning.

It's the reason why one person could see a 120lb female and think she's the most attractive person in this world, yet another person will think she's too skinny and prefers someone that is bigger.

It's the reason why one person could see a man with ripped abs and find him extremely sexy, yet another person will be turned off by his leanness and would much prefer someone who isn't so muscular.

Height, age, hair style and color, complexion, how you talk, how you walk, your smile, your teeth – all of these things will be seen differently by everyone. No two people in this world will ever see you the exact same way.

Yet here you are – the same exact person. There is only one single physical representation of you, yet there are infinite ways people see you.

The way people see you has nothing to do with you. It has everything to do with them. So the version of you they've created in their mind is not your responsibility to manage.

They've had a lifetime of experiences involving parents, family, friends, coworkers, and society that have shaped their worldview.

They have beliefs on what's beautiful, moral, smart, and worthy, and that's the lens through which they see the world.

When that lens comes across something or someone that's out of focus, it creates a form of discomfort. This discomfort is "vocalized" through verbal/mental judgments and behaviors.

If that person received a lot of praise and attention at a certain weight or hair color, there's a very good chance those associations will be projected onto other people. They will see what they know, what they've experienced, and how they felt.

HANDLING JUDGMENT

If a friend got bullied for her weight when you were younger, then you're going to associate weight with pain. You'll see representations of that pain in the real world everywhere.

That doesn't mean everyone will see these people just like you do. They have their own lenses, and they will perceive people differently than you.

Some people will compliment you – others will criticize you. Of course, it feels good to receive these compliments, but again, they have nothing to do with you. Their compliment is packaged with their unique perspective.

This is very empowering to understand because the same goes for criticism. Criticism is just a reflection of that person's life experiences. It has nothing to do with you, so there's no need to take it personally.

The very same person can be both complimented and criticized on the very same body features by different people. That's proof that there is no absolute truth to who you are in other people's eyes.

Compliments and criticisms are opinions, and opinions aren't truths. It's the reason why we shouldn't become dependent on validation from others. The more we tie our self-worth to other people's opinions, the more we'll live for compliments and die from criticisms.

Remember, your appearance isn't absolute – it is relative to each individual person and their life experiences. And one of those individuals is you.

You get to decide who you are, what you look like, and whether you're attractive. So instead of devoting so much energy to trying to impress strangers who will all see you differently and who will likely never be a part of your life, why not work on the relationship that matters most – the one person you have to see and experience life with every single day?

That person is you. Define your own truth. Decide your own self-worth. Live your true life experience. Because the only person's opinion of you that matters is your own. And whatever you believe is right.

Who Cares

My mom passed away a few months before I started writing this book.

After her passing, I didn't post much on social media. I pulled away from life in general. And I spent time grieving my loss and processing my thoughts.

But I did have a major takeaway from that experience I'd like to share with you, so that maybe you can see life in a new way.

After my mom had her stroke, she began a 4-month downhill journey. Her personality instantly changed, then it turned to hallucinations, memory and time distortion issues, and eventually, she stopped talking altogether.

I remember sitting at her bedside a few months into this experience, looking at her suffering, and thinking, "none of this stuff I worry so much about really even matters".

I would give anything to rewind my life just a few short months so that I could focus on the time and relationship I had with my mom.

Instead, I've spent so much of my life worried about my body, my insecurities, and not living my full life experience because I was afraid of failure, judgment, and rejection.

HANDLING JUDGMENT

I looked at my mom and just thought, "WHO CARES!"

The only things that matter are the connections you make and the life you live, yet so many of us are getting in our own way of that experience.

So now, anytime I'm feeling resistance to doing something I want to do, I just say, "WHO CARES!"

My pants are tight? WHO CARES!

You're nervous about giving a speech? WHO CARES!

You're worried about people judging you? WHO CARES!

You're afraid someone will say no if you ask for what you want or need? WHO CARES!

When it's my turn to have my final months of life, none of this is going to matter. I don't want a bag of regrets to deal with.

One of the final coherent things my mom said before she passed was, "I really got myself into a pickle" and "I don't want to lose you all".

Well… life is finite, so do what you want without a worry in the world, because – WHO CARES!

CHAPTER 9

BODY ACCEPTANCE

Body vs. Body Image

What most people think is a body problem is actually a body image problem. They feel bad about the way they look and they think the solution is in changing their bodies. But in reality, that's just a roundabout way of trying to fix your body image. The problem with that path to feeling better about yourself is that it keeps your body image tied to your physical body.

Your body is what you see, while your body image is what you perceive. Your body is simply your physical body. It is rational and objective. It is observed without judgment. If you have fat, you have fat. If you have cellulite, you have cellulite.

On the other hand, your body image is how you perceive your physical body. It encompasses beliefs and feelings about how you look. It is emotional and subjective and rooted in judgment. If you have fat, then you ARE fat. And fat means something to you – usually pain, shame, or a loss of self-worth. If you have cellulite, then that means something about you, such as you're ugly, disgusting, and need to be hidden at all costs.

For most people, their body and their body image are one and the same. This means that their body image is 100% dependent on their physical body. In order to feel better about themselves, be more confident, have more self-worth, accept themselves, or respect themselves, it requires them to change their physical body.

That doesn't mean that you shouldn't focus on your physical body at all. What it means is that if you feel physically bad about your body, in other words, it is negatively impacting your health and keeping you from doing the things you want to do, then by all means you should work on taking care of it in a way that makes those things more possible.

However, if you emotionally feel bad about your body, then you need to separate your body from your body image and work on your body image independently of your physical body. That way they are both getting the attention they need, and you are maximizing their interdependent relationship.

Don't just expect your body image to improve just because your body changes. It can, but your body and body image become so tied together that for you to feel happy, confident, and valued, you need your body to always be a certain size. You remain obsessed with trying to be smaller, and you live in fear of being any bigger.

There are people who lose weight and end up becoming even more critical of their bodies, and there are those who gain 10lbs but love how they look even more.

You can be confident and have an amazing body image inhabiting any sized body. You can also be in a culturally ideal body and be miserable, critical, and so afraid of judgment that you end up not living your full life experience.

Body image can't be seen by other people, so don't assume that just because someone has a body you want that they must also be happy. I've spoken to enough people who tell me that they put on a good front for other people, while inside they are struggling with their appearance. And don't assume that because someone is in a stereotypical bigger body that they must be miserable. These are your own body image projections.

Physical changes aren't necessary for you to improve your body image and start feeling better about your appearance. The best thing about your body image is that it is perception and opinion, and both of those can be changed without a single change to your body. In other words, you can start feeling better about yourself today.

Even better, as you start feeling better about yourself, that affects how you go about eating and moving your body. Food struggles tend to be inversely correlated to your body image. In other words, the worse your body image, the more you tend to struggle with food. Therefore, improving your body image is a prerequisite to transforming your relationship with food.

Your body image determines how much you eat, what you eat, why you eat, how consistent you are, whether you are in a permissive state, your obsessive thoughts around food, and everything else.

With a negative body image you restrict, deprive, distrust, and see calories and hunger as liabilities. It holds your eating hostage, keeps you in a food prison, and forces you into decisions that aren't in your body's best interest. There's always an eating bias towards eating less and being smaller, which makes it hard to heal your relationship with food.

With a positive body image you honor, satiate, satisfy, nourish, and see food as an asset. You stop using food to control your body and the way you feel about it, and instead start using it to address your mental, emotional, and physical needs of the moment. Satiated and satisfied feels much different when you love and accept your body versus when you hate and reject it.

So, drive a wedge between your body and your body image. A lifetime of Diet Culture, societal beauty standards, sneaky marketing, life experiences, and limiting beliefs have led you to believe they are one and the same and that your body image can't be changed unless you change your body first. That is false, and it keeps you from accepting yourself as you are – as a valued human being with inherent self-worth.

Living Your Full Life Experience

A good friend asked if I'd like to come over and swim. To a normal person, this sounds like fun. In Texas, where the summer temps routinely hang out over 100 degrees, a pool is a nice reprieve from the heat.

But I'm not normal. The word "pool", just like the word "presentation", used to cause me immediate anxiety. Why? Because I was afraid of being judged. Afraid of what people would think of my body. Afraid I wouldn't live up to expectations. After all, I'm a fitness coach, and in my head, every ounce of fat is a red mark on my permanent record.

So what did I do? I did what any sane person would do. I spent the day before the party outside without a shirt on. The goal was to get a nice little sunburn. That way, I had a great excuse for keeping my shirt on at the pool party. After all, it would be really dumb of me to expose my already sunburned skin to yet more sunshine.

But the avoidance behavior wasn't just limited to pool parties. It kept me from going to the beach, my favorite place in this world. It kept me from going to the gym more times than I care to admit. It has destroyed friendships because I wouldn't leave the house, as I was too afraid to show myself after gaining weight. And it affected my closest relationship.

"Don't touch me!" Those were the words that commonly came from my mouth at the apex of my body image struggles. They were mostly directed towards my wife, who became an affected bystander of my insecurities. Her hands around my stomach or sides sent deep feelings of insecurity and shame throughout my body, and the only way for them to be released was through the words – "don't touch me there."

My insecurity quickly led to fewer and fewer hugs and intimate moments, as she was afraid of doing something that might upset me. What my body felt like to her as she put her arms around me with feelings of love never even crossed her mind. It only mattered to me. I was never able to see through the insecurity so that I could share in the loving moment.

You can see how a negative body image can keep you from living your full life experience. And not to make you feel worse, but you aren't the only one that's affected as a result of how you see yourself. In my case, my family didn't get to go on those beach vacations or spend as much time at the pool. And obviously, my wife lost the ability to fully connect with me.

I have had to talk so many clients through the idea of going on a vacation where they have to wear a swimsuit. Each of them was extremely anxious about the possibility of being judged by others. But after a shift in perspective, they all were so glad they went. They had the courage to not let their body image get in the way of their life experience.

That's what we're really trying to accomplish here – living a full life experience. That means getting our physical bodies to a place where we can move in the way we want and do the things we want to do. And it means getting our psychological bodies, aka our body image, to a place where our thoughts don't create avoidance behaviors and keep us from doing the things we love.

The Misery Gap

Most of us live in what you'd call the misery gap. This is the space between where you are and where you want to be. In terms of your body, it's the gap between the body you have and the body you desire – usually some kind of societal ideal.

It's no fun being in the misery gap. You're kind of in no-man's land. You're neither happy with the body you have, nor have you achieved the body you want. You're just kind of "there," floating through space – letting life pass you by as you live in a state of discontent.

Some people's misery gap is huge. The space between what they currently look like and what they desire to look like is so large that hope is crushed. But despite having little hope, they still spend their entire life in Diet Culture chasing after minimal success rates.

You don't want to live in the misery gap. After all, you're miserable there. But more importantly, it's hard to get out of it once you put yourself in it. Why? Because the thoughts and behaviors that encompass the identity of someone stuck in the misery gap just reinforce the misery. You put yourself into this prison and then you put a lot of effort into keeping yourself there. It feels like you're trying to get out. You're trying to lose weight and achieve society's ideal body. But you never get there. Perpetual dieting becomes your norm. And this just becomes your life.

The good news is you don't have to stay in this prison. You put yourself in it and you can let yourself out. But you won't get out of the misery gap so long as you reject your current body and put the societal ideal up on a pedestal.

You have to deleverage your belief system. You have to close the gap. You have to minimize the space between how you feel about your body now and what you think it should look like.

That means you approach this problem from two fronts – the first through body acceptance, and the second through managing body expectations.

Body acceptance is the antidote to body rejection, body hate, and negative self-talk. Most people think the solution is changing your body, but that's the very thinking that threw you into the misery gap in the first place.

Acceptance is essential to your success. The behaviors that are born from a place of self-acceptance are much different than the ones born from a place of rejection and self-hate. When you value yourself more, you take care of yourself. Your behaviors then move away from body control and are approached from a place of self-care. The latter means you act in a way that's in alignment with your body's needs. You choose behaviors that make you feel your best. Rejection leads to you engaging in diet culture behaviors that have nothing to do with meeting your body's needs. Instead, you act from a place of fear and misery that just leads to inconsistency.

As you work on body acceptance, you'll also need to work on changing your body expectations. By moving closer to body acceptance and by challenging your body expectations, you close the misery gap and get yourself out of the prison of suboptimal life experience.

Body expectations are changed by exploring the value you've placed on having a particular body. You have formed beliefs about what is beautiful, what is valuable, and what you need to look like to feel worthy in society. These beliefs are not facts. They are conditioned opinions that have been internalized over and over again until they feel like truth. But these beliefs are not universal laws of truth, so they can be changed.

We define the new Ideal Body as the body you're in when you've healed your relationships with food, body, exercise, and mind. It's the body you're in when you've done what is possible based on the unique confines of your personality, circumstances, psychology, and genetics. It's the body you're in when you're happy, healthy, confident, and living your full life experience because you're choosing to run your operating system using an empowering belief system.

When you choose to accept your body and focus on healing your relationships with food, body, exercise, and mind, the misery gap narrows, and you're able to act from a more effective and empowering place. You will never achieve what you desire by keeping yourself in the misery gap. Only by closing the gap can you live your full life experience.

The Double Standard

We want people to love us. We want people to respect us. We want people to accept us unconditionally. We even get mad and upset when they don't do these things. Yet we won't even do those things for ourselves.

How do you expect other people to love, respect, and accept you and your body if you aren't willing to do it yourself? We keep trying to change our bodies so that we can earn value, increase our self-worth, and finally feel worthy of acceptance. Yet in the meantime, we live in a state of hate, disrespect, and rejection.

If this is how you choose to treat yourself, and make no mistake, it is a choice – then don't expect others to embrace you unconditionally. We teach people how to treat us by modeling our own standards. If you have low standards for yourself, others will fall to meet your standards.

When you don't love yourself, you teach others how to not love you. When you don't respect your body, you teach others how to not respect your body. When you don't accept yourself unconditionally, you teach others how to only accept you conditionally.

You need to be your own role model. We're all looking to other people to set the standards for the way they will see and treat us.

But you don't need to rely on others to feel better about yourself. You can take your own stand and start expecting new standards from yourself.

There is zero reason to not accept yourself unconditionally. Zero. Every reason you have for rejecting your current body is rooted in a limiting belief.

Accepting yourself unconditionally is not the same thing as giving up on yourself. It doesn't mean you'll never change. It doesn't mean you won't lose weight. It means that the change that happens will come from a place of self-love and compassion. And frankly, it's the only kind of change that truly works.

We think this rejection of our body is harmless, or worse, we think it helps us lose weight and feel valued. Yet most people struggle to accept themselves unconditionally and continue to struggle with their weight and body. You can't hate yourself into a smaller body while also improving your life experience.

Achieving your Ideal Body is a side effect of body acceptance. It's not the cause of it. It happens as a side effect of healing your relationship with your body. You can't reject yourself into reaching your Ideal Body. All you end up with is a smaller body (maybe) and the same self-hate, criticism, negative self-talk, and self-worth tied to your body. All this baggage just comes along for the journey. It doesn't go away simply because you lose a few pounds.

Body acceptance starts with you, and it also starts you on the right path to your Ideal Body journey. Embracing who you are and what you look like in any given moment is what improves your life experience. Your body changing is just the side effect of that newfound self-respect and acceptance.

BODY ACCEPTANCE

Acceptance Isn't Giving Up

Acceptance of who you are and what you look like starts today – not at some future date once you look a certain way.

This is one of the hardest things for people to do or even accept. The simple thought of accepting a body that has created so much pain elicits all sorts of negative feelings.

I've had people get angry at me at the mere suggestion of acceptance. There's annoyance, dismissiveness, frustration, and confusion. But this is all because of a misunderstanding of what acceptance means for you now and for your future.

When you don't accept yourself, you're actually pushing yourself away. You're rejecting who you are today, even though there's nothing about this moment that can be changed. This moment is all we have. Your future beyond any given moment is not guaranteed. So rejecting yourself and waiting until a non-guaranteed future date just means you're going to be in pain every step of your journey until you reach your goal.

Is this what you want? Do you want to live 24/7 with someone you dislike and reject? What about in real life? If you were living with someone you didn't like, or you had a neighbor that bothered you or created resistance every moment of every day, what would the quality of your life be?

And how do you treat the people in your life that you love and accept vs the ones you dislike and reject? Who do you take care of more? Who do you want to spend your time and energy with? Who creates more happiness in your life?

Acceptance is not giving up on yourself. Continuing down the same weight-obsessed path for 30 more years is giving up on yourself. Acceptance is the first step to changing who you are and is the greatest form of self-care there is. As soon as you choose to accept yourself as-is today, without any conditions, it will be the moment you feel in alignment and at peace with who you are. Your journey will be more enjoyable, and the actions you take will come from a place of self-care instead of from a place of self-hate.

Acceptance is not complacency. It does not mean you're burying your head in the sand. You absolutely can want to change yourself. Acceptance and change are not mutually exclusive goals. They work together. You accept yourself for who you are today and you get excited about the person you will become. And then you enjoy every step of your journey – accepting yourself every moment of it for where you are.

I've approached my own journey both ways – from a place of rejection and shame, and also from a place of acceptance and self-respect. I'm not going to lie, the first way did get me some weight loss. But I was miserable the entire time. I was never good enough or looked good enough. Surrounding yourself with a cloud of body shame is a horrible way to live. I learned very quickly that self-hate can't be overcome with food and exercise. It has to be smothered with acceptance.

When I approached my journey from a place of acceptance, I got to enjoy all the positives of experiencing a future outcome – today. From day one, I felt peace, confidence, and was able to live my full life experience. I didn't put my life on hold until I looked a certain way. I went to the beach. I went to the pool. I went out in public without fear of judgment or not feeling worthy enough to just be me.

There are a lot of people who will say that acceptance is the easy way out of your pain – that it's a way around doing the hard work of changing your behaviors and body. This couldn't be further from the truth. Your journey of self-acceptance will be one of the hardest things you do. Changing your physical body is easy compared to having to reprogram the thoughts and perspectives you have surrounding who you are and how you perceive yourself.

BODY ACCEPTANCE

All I can tell you is this – acceptance is the single greatest thing you can do for your transformation. Whether it happens now or in the future, it will be the thing that brings you peace. No amount of physical body change will do that for you alone. You can't change your internal state through external means.

So yes – work on your body if it means you're going to feel healthier and will have a higher quality of life, being able to live all the experiences you want. But independently of that, accept yourself for who you are and what you look like from day one of your journey. Be proud of who you are and get excited about who you will become.

PART III:

RELATIONSHIP WITH EXERCISE

CHAPTER 10

PERMISSION-BASED EXERCISE

Do What You Want

I've been lifting weights for nearly 30 years. I started training when I was 12 years old. And excluding a few short periods over those decades, I pretty much worked out 3-4 days per week all of my life. You could say that lifting weights had become a part of my identity. I just did it.

But sometime in my later 30s, I started to have some real motivation struggles when it came to getting out and doing my workouts. For whatever reason, I just wasn't enjoying it much anymore. It started feeling like an obligation I needed to fulfill – a should do, instead of an "I want to do."

Workouts started getting inconsistent, and I would literally stand at my back door and look out the window trying to convince myself to go outside and work out (my home gym is on my back patio, by the way).

My workouts had become an obstacle. And every time I pushed myself to do one, it didn't make them easier to do, it made each time more difficult – essentially reinforcing the idea that I was starting to hate what I was doing.

Piggybacking off the idea of Permission-Based Eating, I decided to lower the intense feelings I was experiencing around exercise by giving myself permission to do whatever exercise I wanted to do, in as much quantity, whenever it felt good to do it.

This permission, just like with food, brought up all kinds of limiting beliefs. I can't not strength train... I'll lose my muscle. Is walking really enough? Can I be healthy and fit just working out a few times per week?

The fear-based pull to run back to my strength training was strong. But instead of falling back into the cycle of negative workout experiences reinforcing my loathing for working out, I leveled my beliefs and started fresh.

What did I want to do? Was there anything I've always wanted to try but felt like it wouldn't be good enough for some reason? How much exercise sounded good to me? Should I train every day or just a few times per week?

What I ended up settling on was to commit to 100 days of no strength training. Instead, I was going to do my daily morning walks, which I absolutely loved doing, and I was also going to try my hand at some daily yoga – yes... yoga, the thing I once arrogantly told people was just a warmup for my real workout.

I bought a mat and subscribed to a yoga app, and I went at it. And it lasted – a week. Why? Well for starters, I didn't really enjoy yoga all that much. But more importantly, I was really missing lifting weights.

The absence of strength training from my life showed me just how much I actually enjoyed it. Giving myself full permission to do any kind of exercise I wanted severed the negative association I was having with strength training and allowed me to see it for what it really was – something I actually did enjoy, that helped me feel strong and empowered, and was a part of who I was and wanted to continue being.

That's what permission does. It moves you away from shoulds and have tos and allows you to see your true wants and desires. Getting to that place is the key to staying motivated to doing something for life.

I went back to lifting weights, feeling grateful that I had a home gym and was capable of expressing movement of my body in that way. And anytime I feel motivation waning to lift weights, I remind myself that I have full permission to do anything I want. With that mental framework, I know exactly what I want to be doing and what I'm going to enjoy most.

What Are the Benefits?

We're a very results-driven society. Most of the things we set off to do are because we want to achieve something in the future. That thing could be physical, such as money, weight loss, or better health, or it could be psychological in nature, like feeling more confident or more valued in society.

Essentially, everything we do is just a means to an end. The behavior we implement is something we put up with in order to get the reward at the end of the rainbow. It's a necessary evil.

We even go so far as a society to attach certain meaning to this kind of mindset. We glorify this idea of discipline, and we shame the idea of instant gratification. We create sayings like "good things come to those who wait" – anything to help us justify the discomfort we feel on the journey to some promised outcome in the future.

Article after article touts the "benefits" of doing said thing. Because we think that's what's going to motivate us to tough it out and do what needs to be done to achieve those rewards. And why wouldn't it motivate us? The benefits sound amazing. Who wouldn't want reduced stress, less anxiety, more peace, better health, a more fit body, more muscle, more strength, a smarter brain, slowed-down aging, or any number of the other amazing benefits of exercise?

No one reads those articles and all the touted benefits and says "no thanks, I'm good". Instead, everyone says "I want that", and then they proceed to engage in behaviors they really don't enjoy, but are willing to tolerate to get those benefits.

This is what you call the "what are the benefits syndrome". This syndrome actually takes you further away from the benefits, as it leads you to overlook the essential thing that best drives all behaviors and consequential outcomes – enjoyment.

Enjoyment is what gets you up in the morning to exercise. Enjoyment is what keeps you showing up day after day after day. Enjoyment is the gateway into more and different types of exercise. Enjoyment is what allows you to stay engaged with the process long enough to experience all the secondary benefits like less stress, better health, improved brain function, and more fitness. Yes... these are secondary benefits of exercise. The primary benefit? Enjoyment and how that enriches your life in the moment.

When you focus your attention on achieving the primary benefit of enjoyment and experiencing instant gratification, the dozens of secondary benefits manifest naturally. And there's no need to delay gratification. You stay gratified every step of the way of your journey. You don't have to be a martyr. You don't have to be miserable. You don't have to waste away your life to improve your life. You realize your workout is the reward. It is the payoff. And it is happening now.

Ask yourself this question – "if exercise couldn't change your body or your health or lead to any other secondary benefit beyond the 15 minutes to an hour you exercise, what would you do for physical activity?"

Some people would say nothing. And that's understandable when you've been conditioned for a lifetime to believe you have to put up with something you don't really like doing in order to get the benefits you want. But this just shows that there's some healing to undergo in regards to your relationship with exercise. And that starts right here.

Others will have a list of objections. They'll say things like "well I like doing x, but it won't do y for me". They'll think it's not good enough, or that it won't produce the desired benefits. The only problem with that thinking is that not enjoying what you do is a near guarantee that you won't achieve those secondary benefits anyways. Why? Because you won't do it consistently, long enough, to experience them. If you hate the process, you'll never sustain your behaviors long enough to achieve your outcomes.

You don't have to love exercise, but you do need to enjoy it enough that it will pull you to want to do it. All other goals, as we'll get to next, are built upon the foundation of enjoyment.

You can't get the long-term results you want doing exercise you hate, unless you're one of the rare few who get pleasure from being miserable. And that goes for any benefit you're trying to achieve with exercise. Instead, filter out the secondary benefits for a moment and start having fun again. Physical activity is meant to be enjoyable.

The Exercise Selection Pyramid

Enjoyment is the foundation of all your goals. Whether you want to get stronger, build muscle, lose body fat, get healthier, pursue sports, do a pull-up, or run a 5k, all of these outcome-based goals are predicated on you enjoying the underlying behaviors that will lead to them.

Picture a three-layered pyramid. The bottom layer is enjoyment. The middle layer is performance, and the top layer is physique. You will use this pyramid to help you select the best exercise for you and your unique goals.

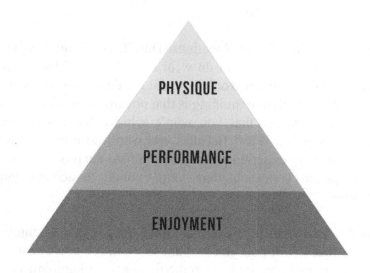

Every level of the pyramid is dependent on you fulfilling the level or levels below it. If any lower layer is not being addressed, then the layers above will start to crumble.

For example, let's say you want to get stronger, so you start lifting weights. Strength is found within the middle layer of the pyramid – performance. In order for you to improve your performance, whether it's strength gains, as is this case, or whether it's endurance, speed, flexibility, agility, etc., the enjoyment layer must be built first.

The reason is very simple – if you don't enjoy the strength training you'll be doing to get stronger, then you won't stick with it long enough to realize your strength gains. Sure, you can willpower your way through it for a little while. But consistency will eventually disintegrate, and you will be back to square one. Your strength training journey will be littered with cycles of extreme consistency followed by a sporadic workout here or there, or none at all.

If the performance layer has to do with all the action-based goals you'd like to achieve, then what is the physique layer? The physique layer incorporates any changes to your body, both externally or internally.

Externally this might mean weight loss, fat loss, weight gain, or muscle gain. Internally would refer to changes to the physiology of your body, such as a more energy-efficient muscle for running, or a healthier body from reduced cholesterol or improved insulin sensitivity.

In order for these physique changes to happen, the two layers of the pyramid beneath it must be satisfied. If even just one is neglected, then the physique changes will not occur.

For example, if your physique goal is to build muscle, you will need a performance-based goal of strength training (the middle layer), which requires you to enjoy that activity – fulfilling the bottom layer of the pyramid. You can't build muscle without the strength training stimulus, and the strength training won't consistently be applied to your life if you don't enjoy what you're doing.

All physique goals are natural byproducts of the two layers below it. They are outcome-based goals, which tend to happen when you are fully engaged with your journey.

This is why you can't just mimic your favorite fitness influencer, health guru, or athlete and expect to get the same result. Yet that is what people do every single time.

They'll see someone's body that they admire and they decide they want that same body. So they see what they're doing for exercise and assume they can just copy them and the result will be the same.

What people don't understand is that the people who have these bodies that you admire got them because they were fulfilling the exercise selection pyramid, whether they realize it or not. They're in the gym lifting weights because they love to lift weights. And their bodies (the physique layer) are just a natural side effect of them fulfilling the two layers of the pyramid beneath it.

When you try to simply mimic what other people are doing, you are working the pyramid backwards. You are starting at the top layer. That's like trying to build the 50th floor of a skyscraper without building the foundation or the floors beneath it. So you copy what they do, and maybe it works for a bit, but the foundation is so shaky that eventually you become inconsistent.

The top of the pyramid starts with the foundation. Your physique goals start with enjoyment. Decide what it is that you like to do and build upon them. If you don't like strength training, then don't expect to achieve a muscular body. If you don't like exercising at all, then don't expect to achieve your healthiest body. If you don't like running, don't expect to complete a marathon.

But here's the kicker, when you understand the pyramid, you can work it. If there's a goal you want to achieve that requires you to do exercise you don't enjoy, you can work on improving your relationship with that particular exercise. Because more times than not, enjoyment is a byproduct of the meaning you've attached to physical activity. So if you can heal your relationship with it and create some empowering experiences from it, you can learn to enjoy it. We'll be working on that in the next chapters.

PERMISSION-BASED EXERCISE

Tolerating Exercise

Be forewarned. There are many coaches, influencers, and credible people with initials after their names that will try to tell you that you don't need to enjoy exercise to do it.

They will tell you that they don't love exercise – that they just tolerate it because they want to look and feel better. They likely have also experienced a lot of weight loss holding onto this belief.

This will be music to your ears. You will feel validated and think – "I don't like exercise either, but I want the results just like him/her, so I will just put up with it and tolerate it too."

The only problem with this mindset is that, through the process of trying to tolerate exercise, most people actually aren't able to tolerate it. They hate it, so they don't do it. It turns out that the influencer succeeding wasn't the norm and that you once again confused the possible with the probable.

This is a very hidden form of Diet Culture thinking. Many people who don't like exercise have come to accept that it's OK as long as it gets them to the end. This idea of a miserable means justifying an end has become so normalized, that some people will even laugh at the idea of someone saying a very common-sense thing such as, "you should enjoy moving your body."

You absolutely should enjoy something that consumes upwards of 10% of your waking life for the rest of your life. Why are you willing to go through life not enjoying something that takes hours of your days?

Look... you don't have to love exercise. You don't have to romanticize it or make it a passion of yours. Although that would certainly make motivation and consistency very easy for you.

All you need to do is find a way to make it more enjoyable – enough so that you feel a pull to do it. Because simply tolerating exercise, and especially hating it, will not be enough for the majority of people to feel motivated to do it. You will not consistently do what you don't enjoy. How often, when given the choice, do you do things you don't like to do? Regardless, what's the point in having a miserable journey just to have a chance at a future payoff that may or may not ever materialize?

You don't have to put up with something for the rest of your life because you think you have to in order to be happy and fulfilled. This is not a healthy relationship with exercise. You wouldn't tolerate a toxic relationship with a person for the rest of your life, so definitely don't do it with exercise.

Remember… just because you know someone that has achieved the results that you want while not enjoying exercise, it doesn't mean that will be the likely outcome for you. Nothing is impossible. There will always be evidence out there to validate your struggles or desires. And you will find it and choose to overestimate its application to your own life.

Anyone can learn to enjoy moving their body. And the first step is to break this mindset of tolerating exercise that is rooted in Diet Culture thinking. It's based on the idea that you must delay gratification, that you have to be disciplined, or even that you're not supposed to like it.

Break the association that exercise is a tool to manipulate your body – to so-called "look better". Sever the idea that exercise's payoff is in the future. Find the joy in mindful movement, the exercise experience, and feeling better right now. Stop doing exercise you hate just to get the body you want. Stop choosing exercise based on what it will do to your body, and start picking physical activity that actually sounds enjoyable to you independently of whether you think it's good enough. If you enjoy it, then it's good enough and it's serving its purpose.

Diet Culture is what teaches you to shun the idea of being content with being happy. It's what brainwashes you to believe you need to be doing more and more of the things you like less and less. It sells you the idea that exercise is the tool for achieving value in society.

If that's what you want, then by all means go and tolerate exercise for the rest of your life. Continue in a toxic relationship that reinforces the idea that your body is your worth. Keep believing that enjoyment is only for the few lucky people.

Or, start believing that you were born to enjoy moving your body. Believe that your body serves as a vessel for you to have enjoyable life experiences. Believe that exercise's payoff doesn't need to be delayed into the future, but that it can serve as a way to enrich your life – right now.

Is It Enough?

Diet Culture teaches you that there are only two types of exercise – strength training and cardio. Never was this more apparent to me than when my new coaching clients would do their initial questionnaire.

One of the questions I asked them was what their favorite kind of exercise was, and 90% of the time it was either strength training or cardio. When I'd follow up with them and ask them what they would enjoy doing for physical activity if weight loss wasn't their goal or if they were the only person in the world, they would usually answer that question much better.

They'd say things like they've always wanted to learn how to dance. Or they like to walk or hike. Or they enjoy swimming. Or they like to ride their bike, rock climb, kayak, play basketball, or ski.

I loved hearing these answers, as it really brought to the surface my clients' passions. They lit up when they talked about them. It excited them.

But then they always had a follow-up question for me – "is that enough though?" Diet Culture had reached back up and snatched them from the good dream they were having.

As they were floating up in happy land, actually enjoying moving their body, Diet Culture was casting out limiting beliefs in the hopes that it could pull you back into the daily drag of exercising to change your body.

That's when all the doubts would come up. Will doing that build muscle? Will that make me healthy? Will I be able to lose weight if that's all I do? Does that burn enough calories?

So they'd burst their little dream bubble of actually doing physical activity they'd enjoy, and instead opt for the exercise Diet Culture teaches them that will shed the fat and build muscle in the least amount of time possible. Ironically, they keep trying to create the perfect workout program they're never going to follow.

It's tough to break these limiting beliefs. We have studies proving to us that one kind of exercise is better than another for losing fat. We have doctors and organizations saying you need a certain amount of intense physical activity to be healthy. You have weight loss coaches plugging you into their standard meal plan plus strength training plus cardio template.

But none of these things consider the psychological influences enjoyment has on your motivation to be active, nor do they consider one of the most fundamental aspects of choosing physical activity – does it make you happy?

How much happiness are you denying yourself in the pursuit of Diet Culture's beauty standards? Physical activity is meant to be fun. It connects you to others. It puts you into a flow state. Its purpose isn't conformism. It's not meant to be reduced down to a tool to manipulate your body and self-worth. So, break the exercise/weight loss association and start moving your body in a way that puts a smile on your face.

Will that "be enough"? No, it will never be enough for Diet Culture standards. You will always be striving for some future benefit you don't have.

But is it enough to improve your quality of life? It absolutely is. And isn't that why we're doing this? Any physical activity makes you healthier. Any physical activity burns calories. Any physical activity builds muscle. Any physical activity makes you more fit. But not all physical activity is enjoyable. So why not do what makes you happy?

Seeing Exercise as a Burden

For many people, there is a negative association with exercise, and this can happen for many reasons. For starters, many people start exercising when they start dieting. And due to the failed nature of diets, they begin to associate exercise with failure and misery.

Exercise starts off fun while you're motivated, but the dieting and calorie restriction slowly but surely result in less energy and less drive to exercise. It's like trying to drive more on less fuel. Eventually, you just don't want to, or can't, exercise anymore.

Another reason is we've been conditioned to view exercise as punishment. In schools growing up, we were forced to run laps or do pushups when we were bad. One day, my daughter came home and said if she didn't get something signed, she would have to run laps. I asked her, "What's wrong with running laps?" And she said she hated running.

Now, before she started school, she used to beg my wife and me to come with us to the stadium track. As a 5-year-old, she was

159

doing sprints down the track with us and running stairs. I'm not even kidding. She thought it was fun. But once school associated exercise with punishment, she didn't like it anymore. Suddenly, exercise hurt.

Many of us still have the associations with exercise from our childhoods. Maybe your parents told you to exercise because you were overweight, or maybe you do it because you hate your body. Whatever the case, when exercise takes on these negative connotations, it makes it less likely that you'll willingly do it.

If you have a negative association with exercise, then your first step is to create a more neutral environment surrounding it. You'll do that by not thinking of it as exercise anymore and instead start seeing it as movement. That's all you're really doing with exercise anyways – expressing movement of your body, and hopefully, there's an enjoyment component to it too.

And then you let go of the ideas that you have to do a certain amount of it for it to be worthwhile, or that you have to do a particular type of exercise for it to be effective. You're going to do whatever sounds good to you, for however long you like, as many times as you want to.

Exercise is about you. No one is forcing you to do it. You don't even have to do it to lose weight. Your only goal is to work towards finding joy in physical activity again. Once you get to the point that you're moving your body consistently again simply because it feels good, that's when you can visit those performance and physique goals.

In the meantime, the priority is breaking the negative associations you have with exercise. Look at this relationship closely and with an open mind, though. Most of us do have remnants of past negative ties to exercise. Old or even current experiences that involve exercise and punishment, no pain no gain mentality, injuries, lack of results, or simply not liking what you're doing can all be subconsciously influencing your relationship with exercise.

CHAPTER 11

MINDFUL MOVEMENT

State Change

I was in a bad mood. All morning, I felt like I couldn't snap myself out of it. Every little thing was bothering me. There was really no reason for it. My mind just felt consumed by negativity, and I was finding fault in everything.

Unfortunately, Deanna inserted herself into my mental stream of negativity by doing something she never should have – she talked to me.

My internal negative state then got projected outwards, and an argument commenced. I have no idea what it was about. But I'm 100% sure it was dumb. It was just my mind attaching onto something in order to quench its need to feel validated.

This bickering went on for hours – until I put an end to the text argument going on from separate rooms of the house and decided to work out.

After just a 30-minute workout, I was a new person. Getting my heart rate up and moving my body snapped me out of the negative mental state I was in. The change in behavior had created new thoughts and emotions.

I apologized to her before my workout was even done. I had been caught up in this negative state for half the day, and a 30-minute workout made me do a full 180.

It's these kinds of experiences you have to start recognizing if you want to attach new meaning to physical activity and heal your relationship with exercise.

These experiences are what help you find the intrinsic value in moving your body. They change you – not by making you stronger, faster, or more muscular, but by changing how you mentally and physically feel. You get the benefits now. There's no need to delay gratification. The reward is instant.

Right now, you likely see working out as a means to an end. Exercise equals calories burned equals weight loss.

And while there is, of course, some truth to that equation on paper, the math still has to be played out in real life, which requires you to consider many of the psychological influences on exercise.

If much of the association you have with exercise is all about body manipulation, weight loss frustrations, and lack of enjoyment, then you are going to find it very difficult to consistently engage in physical activity long enough for future outcomes to manifest.

A miserable means rarely takes you to an enjoyable end. So you need to find ways to create new empowering experiences with exercise – moments you can draw on for motivation when your desired outcomes aren't coming fast enough or fulfilling your expectations.

One of the ways you can create these new experiences is by recognizing the ways that exercise changes your mental state. On any given day, a good workout can neutralize stress and anxiety, boost your mood, improve your confidence, create a "high", and even take you from a negative body image day to a positive one.

Most of the time, our thoughts lead to emotions, which lead to behaviors. And then these behaviors feed back into our thoughts and emotions – creating either an upward spiral of positive thoughts and behaviors or a downward spiral of the opposite. But you can also insert yourself into that thought/emotion/behavior cycle at the behavior point by working out and creating a state change.

Each time you recognize positive changes in your attitude, energy, or enjoyment as a result of working out, your experience is automatically added to your mental motivation bank, which helps you reinforce the intrinsic value of physical activity. You're continually reminded that you don't have to wait for the payoff – the workout is the payoff.

And you still get all those secondary benefits like improved health, strength, etc., because you're more likely to enjoy the process and stay engaged with it long enough to experience them.

Cultivate the Mind / Body Connection

In order to be able to recognize the changes in your mental and physical states and enjoy the instant and intrinsic gratification of physical activity, you have to be connected to your body. This can be really difficult for some people since exercise has never really been about the now – it's always been a means to a better future.

But as I've mentioned countless times, your desired future is simply the result of you consistently meeting your needs of the now. And one of those needs is having a pleasant exercise experience.

MINDFUL MOVEMENT

Most of us recognize the negative states our body is in. States of anxiety, stress, and low energy are easy to identify with. It's easy to become one with your body in those instances. What isn't as easy for many people is to be self-aware and present enough to notice the positive state your body is in during and after exercise. This takes some practice, but the more in tune you are with your body, the more you can reap the benefits of movement.

What you want to do is try to recognize the different sensations in your body around the periods of heightened physical activity. What happens to your body? What changes? What do you notice about your breathing? What about your heart rate? Do you feel any tingling in your arms or legs? Does your brain feel like it's been stimulated?

Have you ever felt a runner's high? What about a pump in your muscles when you're lifting weights? Did the exercise you just did calm you? Or did it give you more energy? Did it build confidence? Did it change your mood?

Close your eyes right now. See if you can notice and feel your heartbeat. Try to feel it not just in your chest but all throughout your body. Pretend like there's a little you sitting in your head monitoring your body and your thoughts. This is your self. Now pay attention to your breathing. Watch the air fill your lungs and leave through your nose on each breath. Listen to the sounds of your body.

Some people practice this through meditation. That's a great practice and something I do and recommend for everyone. But whether you choose to do it or not, the goal is still the same – cultivate the mind/body connection.

When that connection is strong because it was built through conscious intention, it then works subconsciously on autopilot. You become aware of the mental and physical state changes that occur when you move your body either during a workout or simply through functional movement. And each time you move your body, you get a dose of satisfaction.

This happens once the negative associations and meaning that are currently attached to exercise are stripped away. Only then can you get in touch with movement's true nature. That might sound kind of out there to you, a little woo-woo maybe. But ask yourself whether you're currently getting as much joy from movement as you'd like. And if you're not, be open-minded to ditching the surface level "exercise is a body manipulation tool" mentality and instead start turning inwards and connecting to yourself on a deeper level.

This connection with your body is what drives you to want to move your body for the sheer joy of it. It gives you the instant payoff. And it's what keeps you coming back for more.

Intensity Matters

How hard you exert yourself during your workouts matters. But that doesn't mean pushing yourself to your limits is always the right thing to do. Sometimes pushing too hard can cause unwanted side effects in enjoyment, experience, and how you feel mentally and physically. This is why the "no pain, no gain" mentality is actually hurtful. Because there are plenty of times where the pain leads to no gain – especially when it creates resistance to you wanting to work out because it makes you miserable.

The same goes for not pushing yourself enough. It's entirely possible to under-exert yourself and not feel any of the benefits of mindful movement. So you work out, but it doesn't really feel like you did anything. Neither your body nor your mind were stimulated, so no state changes were experienced. Without them, it becomes difficult to find the intrinsic value in the physical activity you're doing, and motivation suffers.

Mental and physical state changes happen at both the low intensity and high intensity areas of the spectrum, and everything in between. And each type of physical activity you do has its own unique profile and what I like to call an "exertion tipping point".

Each type of movement you do has its own bell curve. There's both a minimum and a maximum level of exertion that leads to a desired state change, and somewhere in the middle is the optimum spot.

And this bell curve isn't static – it's dynamic based on certain variables you bring into the movement experience. The time of day that you work out will influence this bell curve and its exertion tipping point. So will the mental and physical state you're in when you enter into that particular physical activity.

This is why it's so important to cultivate the mind/body connection and to work with your body instead of trying to fit it into a cookie cutter workout program. Some days you're going to have more energy. And others you're going to have less than ideal conditions. Regardless, if you are in touch with your body, you can move your body in a way that makes you feel good, and leaves you in a better mental and physical state than when you started.

So what is exertion anyways? The way I define it is very simple. It's a function of both your workout duration and its intensity. In other words, how long you work out, and how hard you work out. And both these variables can be experimented with in order to give you the optimum workout experience.

For example, I greatly enjoy my morning walks. And one of the reasons why I enjoy them is because of the mental and physical state changes they create.

My walks are leisurely and one of the first things I do after waking up. I'm not powerwalking. I'm walking at a normal pace. I'm not checking my heart rate or doing any kind of performance based measuring.

Before starting my walk I'm still not completely awake. My mind is not firing at 100%, and my body definitely isn't ready to tackle intense physical activity. But after my walk, my mind and body are feeling fresh and ready to tackle the day. I'm ready to sit down and start writing, or even do a more intense strength training workout.

My walk changed my mental and physical states. It primed me for having a great day. But notice how it wasn't intense exercise. It wasn't more is better. In fact, it is difficult for me to do intense physical activity so early in the morning. And when I try to do it, it actually has a detrimental effect on my mental and physical states.

For me, at that time of the day, a longer walk at a leisurely intensity hits the sweet spot of that bell curve. When I go for a walk after dinner with Deanna, my walk is shorter. In that instance, a longer walk would also be detrimental to my states. This can always change as time goes on – especially if you end up having an empowering exercise experience that makes you look at the situation differently. So understand that what is optimal is about the now.

Your exertion tipping points and bell curves will look different than mine. Some people like short but intense workouts. Others like their strength training to take a little longer with more rest between sets (less intense).

Your job is to cultivate the mind/body connection so you can find that sweet spot – the spot where you really internalize the intrinsic value of physical activity. Because this is the kind of empowering association you need to cultivate in order to replace the old disempowering one of – exercise equals weight loss.

Physical activity is not a means to an end. It is the end. It just so happens that when you find the intrinsic value in movement, you end up engaging with it more consistently. And when that happens, there are beneficial side effects. But these side effects will always be secondary to the experience itself.

Energy Production

Physical activity should be a net positive when it comes to your energy levels. If it's not, then something is wrong.

Many people who are stuck in Diet Culture end up experiencing a net negative effect on their energy. This happens for many reasons. For starters, they usually go from doing no exercise to suddenly doing daily intense workouts with the flip of a switch. This doesn't give your body or mind enough time to adapt to the sudden stress you're putting your body through. In time, the physical stress accumulated via your workouts outpaces your recovery, and it's easy to end up taking long extended times off from working out altogether due to burnout.

Another reason this net negative energy situation happens is because exercise is normally paired with a calorie-restricted diet when someone is trying to lose weight. Physical activity requires energy, aka calories. And when you're dieting and are in a sudden 500-1000 calorie deficit each day because you want to lose 1-2 pounds per week, it makes it hard to perform at your best. Exercise starts feeling like a chore. Your motivation to get out of bed to do it diminishes, and then you stop doing it. Exercise becomes a drain on your already low energy, and that association becomes ingrained – making it harder and harder to be motivated to work out, especially if your weight isn't dropping.

So long as you see exercise as a way to burn calories, instead of a tool for enjoyment, experience, and to feel good, you will continue to have a net negative energy liability. If you don't feel more energized as a result of your workouts, then you either have a disempowering association with physical activity, you're not eating enough to support that much activity, or you haven't optimized the amount and type of exercise you do, which usually ties back into the association you have with it.

You should feel good after a workout. Feeling nauseous, exhausted, or any other negative sensation is a sign something is off. Yes... there will be one-off workouts where you push yourself to that point. That's going to happen. But it shouldn't be the norm. It can't be the norm. Your body won't let it be the norm. You'll naturally lose the drive to do it unless your fear of gaining weight holds you hostage to doing it. In that case, you're acting from a place of constant fear AND you feel physically horrible doing it – lose/lose.

So start to feel the difference physical activity makes. Just as you eat to feel your best, you move your body to feel your best. If you eat something that doesn't make you feel good, would you keep eating it even if it resulted in weight loss? Hopefully not. But if you're deep in Diet Culture, you very well might. It's the same for exercise. If you're doing something that doesn't feel good, stop doing it. Don't allow the societal pressures of weight loss push you into doing something that doesn't make you happy. Besides... feeling good from exercise is what makes you want to do it. It's what gets you out of bed. The payoff is now. But it's also in the future, because you're actually doing it. And why do you do it? Because it feels good. See how that works?

Intuitive Exercise

Similar to how intuitive eating allows you to eat in a way that works with your body and its feedback, intuitive exercise also allows you to adjust your workouts in real time based on how you're feeling and what your body is telling you.

MINDFUL MOVEMENT

Not every workout you have is going to be amazing. You're not always going to feel up for working out and/or pushing yourself to your limits. In some workouts, you're going to feel strong and invincible, and in others, you're going to contemplate cutting it short and calling it a day.

These are normal ups and downs of exercise. Even if your relationship with exercise is amazing and you thoroughly enjoy the physical activity you do, there's still going to be those days where you feel a little off. And that's when you have to be a little intuitive about your exercise.

Pushing yourself when your body is saying to pull back some is like continuing to eat well past comfortable fullness. Your body is saying to do one thing, yet your mind isn't honoring that signal.

It's hard for some people to pull back with their workouts. There's a little bit of all-or-nothing thinking involved that makes them feel like anything less than an all-out workout is just not worth it.

And let's not get started with suggesting you just not work out today and take the day off. That can really stir up some emotion. Sometimes I don't know what's harder – working out when you don't want to or not working out when you really do.

But look, if you're feeling sick or maybe injured, sometimes just taking a recovery day is what's best in the long run. Maybe you do go ahead and work out, but you just pull back a little bit on how hard you push.

Intuitive exercise isn't just about knowing when to pull back though. It's also about knowing when to push beyond what was originally planned.

Sometimes you plan to only lift a certain amount of weight for your workout, but as you warm up you realize you feel really good. So you end up working out with more weight than was planned. Or maybe you do an extra rep or set.

If you like to run, you've probably had those moments mid-run when you feel amazing and just want to throw in a speedier interval or three. Maybe your easy run pace feels extra easy today. That's the feeling we're looking out for that we want to be intuitive with. We want to start understanding effort, instead of relying solely on the numbers.

And finally, sometimes intuitive exercise means pushing yourself to just do something, anything for some physical activity. You're not always going to feel like working out. There's a fine line between taking the day off because you don't feel good, and pushing yourself to do something so you will feel good.

If skipping workouts isn't the norm but you're feeling really off today, then that's when being intuitive might mean taking the day off. But if you've been missing workouts lately and the lack of physical activity is making you feel bad, then being intuitive and pushing yourself to just do something would be an act of self-care.

If pushing yourself to work out so you can have a good experience doesn't get you out of that cycle, then it's time to explore why that's happening. Maybe it's time to change things up. Maybe you need to get back to what makes you happy. Maybe some disempowering associations, such as calorie burn or body manipulation, have crept back into your workouts. Staying mindful, intuitive, and investigative will help you uncover your truth.

The more you can work with your body, pulling back when you're feeling off, and pushing when you feel something extra is there, the more enjoyable your workouts will be and the better chance you'll have at achieving your goals.

CHAPTER 12

THE EXERCISE EXPERIENCE

Exercise Is a Vehicle

I walk every single morning. It's how I start my day. In fact, I probably only miss 3 days a year at most when it comes to getting in my morning walk.

Rain? Doesn't matter. I bring an umbrella. Cold? I bundle up. Wind? Hate it, but it's not going to keep me from walking. Snow? Hell yes, I'm walking. That's like a vacation down here in Texas.

You might think my dedication to my morning walk means that I love to walk. But I don't. That's easier to understand once you consider I don't like walking on a treadmill, nor would I like pacing around the inside of my house.

When you frame it that way, you realize that much of the exercise we do isn't because we enjoy that particular exercise; it's because we enjoy the atmosphere and experience it creates.

Exercise is simply a vehicle for creating an experience. It's not about what exercise leads to – it's what it does for you in the present moment. In the end, it's the experience that we enjoy that keeps us coming back for more.

For me, my morning walks check all the boxes that allow me to have an enjoyable experience. It's outdoors where it feels open, and I can get fresh air and be with nature. I get an hour of alone time to do whatever I want, which is usually listening to some kind of personal development podcast or audiobook. I get some time without having any responsibilities to anyone other than myself. And I get to see the sunrise every morning, which can be quite spectacular at times.

Of course, it doesn't hurt that walking in and of itself isn't something I loathe. It's pleasant movement for me. It's not crazy high intensity at 6:30 in the morning, so the resistance to doing it is very low. And I even carry my giant mug of green tea around the neighborhood. Yup… I'm THAT guy. I'm so consistent with this exercise that strangers will come out of their homes and wonder what's up if I'm walking at a different time than usual.

The important thing to remember here is that, in order to heal our relationship with exercise, we need to start attaching new meaning to it. We have to stop seeing it simply as a tool to burn calories and manipulate our bodies and self-worth. And understanding that exercise is a vehicle for creating a desirable experience is one of the best ways to attach more empowering meaning to it.

So, think about why you do the exercise you do. There's a good chance that even if you intrinsically enjoy the activity itself, the experience it creates for you is the bigger driver of your consistency and adherence. After all, if you have a bad experience, regardless of whether you like the activity itself, you are very unlikely to keep putting yourself through it.

The more you view movement as having an experience, the more you'll see it as an opportunity for enjoyment, and the more active you will be. The more you view it as a means to an end, the more it will feel like a chore, and the less you'll want to move your body.

THE EXERCISE EXPERIENCE

The Experience Variables

One of the biggest reasons people struggle to stay motivated with exercise is because they are using it as a means to an end. It's essentially just a tool for achieving their desires of the future.

This is an issue because exercise takes a long time for real changes to take place. Not only does it take a long time, but it requires a lot of consistency.

An impromptu workout here or there, or working out once one week and then 5 times another, really isn't going to do much in terms of the outcomes you are seeking. It's better than nothing, but that kind of inconsistent movement is hard to integrate into your life.

You want to be looking at physical activity on a large scale. Not in days, weeks, or months – but years. This is what you call an active lifestyle.

An active lifestyle is about incorporating movement into your day – every day. And that is impossible to do consistently when you only see exercise as a tool to manipulate your body.

Body changes take longer to manifest than your "willpower workouts" can be sustained. And using your workouts as a means to an end takes a disproportional slice of your willpower reserves.

This is why people struggle to stay motivated with exercise. They keep engaging in suboptimal workout experiences without seeing the future payoff. Doing so would lead to any sane person giving up on exercise eventually.

It's not the workouts that lead to your desired future outcomes – it's your experiences that create them. And the more enjoyable those experiences, the more likely you are to manifest the outcomes you want.

But the focus isn't on the outcomes. The focus is on the now. The focus is on understanding what makes a workout enjoyable for you, as that's what keeps you coming back for more. We call these "exercise experience variables," and they are the key to you finding exercise you enjoy.

If you take a close look at the physical activity you do more consistently than others, you will notice some patterns in the experience that's created.

Do you like to work out indoors or outdoors? Do you like to work out by yourself, with a partner, or in a group? Do you like to work out in silence, or with some form of entertainment?

Do you like having autonomy in doing what you want, or do you like to follow a workout program or instructor? Do you like a lot of variety, or do you like consistency and certainty? Do certain times of the day click better with you?

All these variables culminate to create your overall exercise experience. And this experience is what creates your enjoyment, which leads to sustainable motivation, which naturally drives your future outcomes.

Strength training, for example, isn't what you like or don't like. It is simply the vehicle for creating an experience. And that experience is influenced by the variables outlined above.

If I told you to lift weights at 7am, at a freezing gym with a group of 6 people, with nursery rhymes playing in the background, would that be an enjoyable experience for you? Would you be likely to do it consistently for the next year?

What if I asked you to lift weights and gave you the autonomy to do it as you saw fit? So you decided you wanted to work out mid-morning, outdoors, in the calming quiet of nature, by yourself. Would that be an enjoyable experience for you? And if so, would you be likely to do it consistently for the next year?

THE EXERCISE EXPERIENCE

Both of those scenarios involved strength training, but the exercise experience was different for both. As a result, very different outcomes are going to be the result.

So focus less on the outcomes and the actual type of exercise you do. Instead, see exercise as a vehicle for having an enjoyable experience, and an active lifestyle will be the natural side effect.

Exercise Empowerment

Exercise can be a huge source of empowerment for you. It teaches you how to set goals and achieve them. It shows you that you are stronger than you thought you were, and that you can do more than you previously thought.

You become more confident and end up taking more risks. You push yourself out of your comfort zone more. The confidence you gain from breaking through old performance levels can be applied to your life as a whole.

The resilience you build from pushing yourself to finish that race, when everything within you is saying to give up, can be used to more easily overcome life's obstacles. Your discomfort threshold becomes higher, which opens up all kinds of opportunities that were once hidden by fear or pain.

Exercise is more than just lifting weights or doing cardio. It's about breaking through your self-imposed ceilings and proving to yourself that you are capable of more. The human body has amazing potential, and exercise is one of many vehicles that gives you a small glimpse of what that may be.

It shows you that you are in control of your body. That you have the power to change yourself mentally and physically and direct your life. It puts you more in tune with your body. It better connects your physical and mental being, so you can synergistically harness your optimum human experience.

When done correctly, and with the right self-awareness and perspective, exercise can be a tool for personal growth in any aspect of your life. So, start looking beyond just the physical outcomes it can provide and start considering the positive impact it can have on changing your entire identity.

Take squats, for example. I have a love/hate relationship with them. They are hard. But they feel good to me. I'm not averse to doing hard things, but there is definitely resistance when it's time to train my lower body.

Not only do I know that my muscles are going to get pushed to the max for the next 60 seconds when I do a set of squats, but I have to overcome a lot of mental resistance to even getting under the bar and doing them. There's this inflection point that I have to overcome each time. It's similar to forcing yourself to jump into cold water, or doing something you're afraid to do.

But each time I challenge myself and push through that inflection point, I achieve personal growth, and I build my confidence and power. I become a more capable person. It pushes my comfort zone and what I can handle in life. Through exercise, I train myself to be more resilient and to keep moving forward when things feel tough.

This experience helps me associate new meaning to physical activity. It becomes so much more than something you do to manipulate your body and its worth. It becomes a vehicle for bettering my life. And it's this kind of association that makes me want to continue doing it time and time again, independent of what it does to my body.

Most people can look back in their life and remember a moment they've had with physical activity that made an impression. The reason why is because it was a moment in time when you had a leap in personal growth. It made an emotional imprint because it meant something to you. And this meaning, whether you realize it or not, influenced other parts of your life.

THE EXERCISE EXPERIENCE

While I can't guarantee that you've had one of these moments in the past, I can assure you that you can have plenty of them going forward once you detach exercise from weight loss and start seeing the intrinsic value in it.

I have watched people create all new identities for themselves as a result of them completing a marathon, doing a pull-up, setting a PR on a run or with an exercise, or even completing a difficult hike. It was all about what they did in that moment relative to what they previously were capable of. When you surpass a previous identity by reaching into new mental, emotional, and physical territory, you grow. And it's this process that empowers you to feel strong in body and mind.

When Quitting Is OK

I used to be obsessed with Christmas lights. You might as well have called me Clark Griswold.

I also got really into collecting baseball cards. And then there was that time I started to draw all the time.

I can't forget about when I became an amateur astronomer either. Have you seen Saturn's rings?

I've also had my phases with gardening, piano, Spanish, and plenty more.

And guess what? Not all of these things "stuck". Even though I was crazy passionate about them at the time, most of them faded away.

But that's OK! I don't regret my time doing any of these things even though I'm not doing them anymore. They brought a lot of joy into my life, and there are still remnants of them in my identity.

Not every decision you make has to be a lifetime commitment. This is also true when it comes to picking the type of exercise you do. Everyone thinks you have to decide what you're going to do for exercise for the rest of your life.

Strength training? If I start it, I have to do it – forever.

Running? If I start it, I have to do it – forever.

No, you don't! Instead, commit to a lifetime of physical activity, and then go with the flow for whatever sounds good at the time.

That might mean you get really into strength training for a few months, or running, or swimming, or biking, or hiking, or dancing. It doesn't matter. It's all physical activity. And if you enjoy it, it's going to add to your life experience.

Getting rid of the all-or-nothing mindset surrounding exercise is what actually gets you moving your body. It allows you to try new and interesting things that you either might not have ever thought about before, or you assumed it wouldn't be good enough.

Giving yourself permission to just try things is what opens the doors to new and exciting physical activity. The path of an active lifestyle takes many twists and turns. What you do today is unlikely to be the same exact thing you do 20 years from now.

So don't go into this thinking you have to make a forever decision. You don't. Commit to having experiences with your body. Move it and enjoy it. Move on to a new activity when you aren't feeling the passion of the one you're doing. And go deep into the things you become passionate about.

This is what creates a new identity around exercise. You become a sum of your experiences – each phase of your life influencing the next. And at times you circle back around to a past love. But this time you experience it differently, because you're a different person now.

So go with the flow. Commit to moving your body in whatever way sounds good to you. Let go of the long-term commitments to specific types of movement, and instead start seeing your exercise through the lens of an active lifestyle.

Life Integration

We tend to think of exercise as this separate, compartmentalized thing we do. We have our life, and we have our workouts. And at times, these two things can become very different entities. This is unfortunate, as the more we can integrate health and fitness into our day-to-day life so that it simply becomes our life, the better the exercise experience will be.

It might be easier to think of exercise as an active lifestyle, a culture, or even an identity. Physical activity becomes a part of you. When that happens, it's easy to be motivated to work out.

It's the reason why there are people in certain fitness communities who seem obsessed with the kind of exercise they do. It's as if nothing can keep them from doing that thing.

I've seen cross-fitters, runners, bikers, gym-goers, hikers, basketball players, swimmers, and every other kind of fitness character you can imagine integrate these physical activities into their life as a whole. They live and breathe these things. They aren't just things they do a few times per week to be healthy or change their body – they're hobbies and passions.

That's the kind of experience we're trying to create with exercise, or as I prefer to call it – physical activity, as it's movement of every kind, done at any time, that we're looking to make part of our life. When I talk about improving your life experience, this is part of that experience.

But that's hard for some people. Exercise has such a negative association to dieting, body change, and self-worth struggles, that it feels like a chore and an obligation. They have busy lives, or have desk jobs, and can't imagine a world where they'd actually want to work out with that kind of passion.

And that's OK, because you don't have to call yourself a cross-fitter or a biker to create a better exercise experience. All you need to do is start viewing your physical activity differently and try to blur the line between exercise and life.

How can you make these two things one and the same? When you think of your life, in what ideal scenario could you picture physical activity being an integrated part of it? What kind of movement is in your life? What would you look forward to doing? What would enrich your life?

You won't get the right answer if exercise is a synonym for body control or burning calories. You probably won't get the right answer if you think of exercise as a means to improved health either. While physical activity can change your body and impact your health, it's the experience it creates in your life right now that adds to your fulfillment.

Your body and its ability to move provides you with an amazing asset to get the most value out of your life. Exercise doesn't have to be a means to an end. It doesn't have to hurt. It doesn't have to just be a tolerable thing you do. It's a vessel for enjoyable experiences, and the more movement gets integrated into your life simply because it makes you happy, the more you're going to want to do it, and the more you're going to reap all its benefits.

CHAPTER 13

FATIGUE MANAGEMENT

Getting ZZZZZs

I always feel a little weird talking about sleep. It seems like a boring topic to me. When I tell people to make sure they sleep well, I feel like I'm that parent standing over their kid, telling them to eat their veggies. Yet, even though we all know we should be sleeping well, very few people actually are.

This is a big problem. Most people are focused on the 80% of the details that only get them 20% of their results. They focus on tips and tricks and all those little sexy strategies that get you excited to take action and do something different. Because surely, your struggles couldn't be something as simple as sleep issues.

That's where most people are wrong. If I had to rank all the things I talk about in this book from least impactful to your Ideal Body journey to most impactful, sleep would be rated the highest. It is the single greatest fundamental influencer of your progress, yet it is the single greatest neglected aspect of most people's journey. Health basics aren't sexy. But then again, neither are the side effects of not doing them.

Too many people are focused on micromanaging carbs, calories, or protein, when they aren't even getting a consistent 8 hours of sleep each night. That's putting the cart before the horse. It's trying to put the icing on a cake before you've even baked it.

Lack of optimal sleep handicaps your efforts. Everything you do ends up feeling like you have a ball and chain tied to your ankle. Does it prevent you from taking any action at all? In most cases, it probably doesn't. But it does make everything harder – adding unnecessary resistance to implementing optimum thoughts and behaviors.

Sleep is a prime period of recovery for us. It puts us into the necessary state to recover both physically and mentally. It rebuilds muscles and other tissues. It tops up willpower stores for the day ahead. And it keeps beneficial stress from becoming chronic.

Lack of sleep influences your eating choices. When you're sleep deprived, you are more likely to reach for convenience foods that are more calorically dense. You tend to snack more. You have a harder time finding the energy, and thus the motivation, to exercise. You prevent your willpower from being fully refreshed, which means you're running closer to empty all throughout your day. You become less emotionally resilient, which influences your ability to cope with emotional discomfort, which leads to things like emotional eating, decision fatigue, and a general sense of just wanting to go back to your old ways that require less mental and physical demands.

And here's the thing – when I'm talking about lack of sleep or being sleep deprived, I'm not just talking about the quantity of your sleep each night. I'm talking about the quality of that sleep too. Because anything less than optimal adds unwanted resistance. You'd be surprised just how much easier your health and fitness journey becomes, let alone your life, when you prioritize the rejuvenation and recovery aspects of sleep.

So, how much do you need? Well, studies show anywhere from 7-9 hours per night is optimal. Both less and more than that tend to be correlated to negative side effects. However, these numbers are very individual. Just because you're in that range, it doesn't mean that's what's optimal for you.

So how do you tell how much sleep you really need? I like to use the alarm clock test. If you're waking up to an alarm, it's unlikely you're getting enough sleep. That should be obvious. You are interrupting a sleep cycle and jarring yourself awake. Anyone who has ever woken up naturally knows how much better and fresher they feel as a result.

I personally need about 8.25h of sleep each night. So, I'm shutting things down the night before to give me enough time to be asleep by 9:45pm since I wake up at 6am. When I get to bed on time, I tend to wake up naturally sometime before my alarm – anywhere from 5-20 minutes before it. And when that happens, I just get up. I don't need to go back to bed, because I feel fully refreshed and ready to tackle my day.

This is the true definition of sleeping in. Sleeping in is less about the time you wake up, and more about how you feel when you do wake up. And this is influenced by how consistent your sleep schedule is and how long you sleep.

Sure... there's the odd day here or there where I get to bed later than that and I have to wake up to a jarring alarm with less than optimal sleep, but that is the exception to the norm. Most people have that backwards and are getting less than optimal sleep 90% of the time with maybe a day or two on the weekend when they sleep in.

The sleeping in that's currently happening on the weekends, by the way, likely isn't an accurate representation of the real sleep you need. It tends to be exaggerated due to the sleep debt that accumulates throughout the week. As you start to establish a consistent sleep schedule, going to bed and waking at similar times each day, you'll get a much better idea of how much sleep you really need.

It's time to start bringing that refreshed feeling of sleeping in to every single one of your days. The most productive days start, not when you wake up, but when you go to bed the night before. So make sure you are getting off on the right foot. Achieving your goals is so much easier when you aren't fighting against the wind.

Managing Stress

Stress is not a bad thing. In fact, stress is a very good thing to experience. It's the very thing that allows us to grow both physically and mentally/emotionally. Stress only becomes a problem when you don't allow yourself to recover from it, which then leaves stress unchecked and in a chronic state.

There are both physical and mental stressors, and each can be created intentionally and unintentionally.

For example, we've all experienced stress from work or life. This is what you'd call unintentional mental stress. It is the result of you being in situations that create emotional discomfort. You can call it adversity, but most would just call it exhaustion, frustration, annoyance, or anger at your life situation. Regardless, if you allow yourself to recover from these stressors, you become more emotionally resilient to the same stressors over time. When you don't allow yourself to recover from it, it becomes chronic stress, and that can lead to all kinds of consequences – health issues, negative life experiences, the people around you getting the residual side effects of your stress, low energy, and so forth.

But this mental stress can also be intentional. This is what a lot of personal development is, and something you'll be experiencing a lot as you heal your relationships with food, body, exercise, and mind. Intentional mental stress is better known as pushing your comfort zone. You intentionally put yourself into situations that create emotional discomfort in an effort to grow as a person. Maybe you hate public speaking but you do it anyways. Or maybe you have a difficult conversation with a co-worker, family member, or friend over boundaries. Whatever the situation, by pushing your comfort zone, it expands. And after some short-term discomfort, your life as a whole becomes easier and more fulfilling.

Physical stress can also be experienced both intentionally and unintentionally. Intentional physical stress is better known as exercise. That's right, exercise stresses the body. It's the stimulus that forces your body to adapt. Every time you run, your body adapts and gets faster. Every time you lift weights, your body adapts and gets stronger.

But if you leave this intentional physical stress unchecked, it can become chronic, also known as overtraining, or more accurately known as under-recovering. When this stress is chronic, you experience issues like injuries, illness, and motivation struggles.

Finally, unintentional physical stress is simply the movement you experience as part of your life. Maybe you have a demanding job. Or maybe you do a lot of physical work around your home. Whatever the case, periods of recovery are required to balance the stress cycle and keep it from becoming chronic.

How do you do that? Some of it you already do. When it comes to unintentional mental stress, you take vacations and have weekends and nighttimes to recover. Intentional mental stress that is of the personal development nature tends to come in cycles of pushing out of your comfort zone for a while and then recovering within that new expanded zone until you're ready for a new push. Intentional physical stress is recovered from using days off from training during the week, extended occasional deloads, and by managing the amount of fatigue you accumulate on a workout-to-workout basis. And unintentional physical stress tends to also be recovered from in the form of weekends, vacations, and evenings/nights out.

So hopefully you see now that stress isn't a bad thing. Avoiding stress isn't going to help you. All that does is shrink your comfort zone, make your life feel smaller, and forces your body to become weaker and less able to handle the functional needs of life. It's the flip side of stress, aka recovery, that balances this stress cycle and allows you to grow as a person. So don't avoid it. Embrace it. And then balance it with the necessary recovery if you want to thrive.

Resting Is Doing Something

There are two kinds of people in this world: People who have a hard time exercising when they're not motivated, and people who have a hard time not exercising when they are. But really, we all tend to experience both of these scenarios at various times.

I've come to realize that getting people to take some time off from working out when they're extremely motivated to exercise is a difficult thing to do. These people have a lot of limiting beliefs surrounding exercise that prevent them from prioritizing rest and recovery.

I was one of those people. I'm the guy who gets super motivated to try a new strength training program, or to take up running and do too much too fast, only to start feeling some aches and pains creep in. Of course, I ignore them, because I need to keep working out so that I don't lose all my progress. Plus, I'm usually thoroughly enjoying the exercise (minus the aches and pains).

These overuse injuries get worse and worse until eventually, I'm forced to take time off. But at this point, I have to take a much longer absence from exercise in order to heal my body than if I would've just listened to my body and better prioritized rest and recovery.

FATIGUE MANAGEMENT

Not all motivation is good. It's only good motivation if it provides you with a positive outcome. If your motivation drives you into the ground and destroys your body, steals the energy of your day, or keeps you living in fear of losing your results, then that is not good motivation – it is a liability.

I hear all kinds of reasons for not wanting to take enough days off from exercise or not wanting to rest enough in general. But one of the biggest objections is people say they feel like when they don't work out that they aren't doing anything.

Here is what I always say – resting IS doing something. In fact, it's a very difficult something to do for a lot of people.

Your body doesn't grow when you exercise. It grows when you rest and recover. Exercise is only a stimulus for growth. It is not growth itself. That workout you just did? You didn't grow from it. In fact, your body is now broken down and in a weaker state than when you started.

Exercise doesn't build muscle. It breaks it down. It doesn't make you stronger. It actually makes you weaker initially. Nor does it make you faster or give you more endurance. These are all just stimuli for growth. For the growth cycle to complete, it has to be paired with recovery.

We stimulate growth, accumulate fatigue, and then recover and grow. That's the process. If any of those areas are lacking, the growth cycle will suffer. You will get negative side effects such as injuries, illnesses, and stagnant progress. And when any of these things happen, your motivation suffers and potentially causes a chain reaction downstream.

Your routine breaks down and you become inconsistent. Your eating falls off track, and you stop feeling your best. One thing leads to another and you end up going through a period of stagnation or even regression in your personal development journey.

Only you can determine if you're getting enough rest. You don't have to do nothing. Sometimes, reduced volume or intensity is enough depending on your overall fitness level. Even a leisurely walk could be a form of recovery. But if your motivation is rooted in fear, there's a good chance your recovery is suboptimal and you could stand to benefit from more of it.

Remember, operating at high levels of fatigue from unchecked stimulation and stress can negatively affect hormones, mood, thoughts, and behaviors. There are a lot of people who are actually imprisoned by exercise, and their lives reflect that.

Exercise is good for you, and you should find joy in moving your body. But it needs to be paired with recovery for you to have the best experience with it.

Recovery is what builds you back up better, stronger, and faster. Without it, you simply experience the negative side effects of unchecked stress. Every day you intentionally stress your body without allowing it to build itself back up and become more resilient to it.

So don't think for a moment that you're lazy or that you aren't doing anything when you're taking days off from working out. Rest and recovery add to your life experience and make you a stronger person in the end.

Get On the Priority List

Sometimes managing fatigue and optimizing recovery means doing nothing and resting, but other times you are able to recharge yourself by engaging in an activity that creates a flow state. For this reason, it's important that you set aside time every single day that is just for you to do anything that you want.

This me-time is free of most, if not all, responsibility to others, and is used as a form of self-care. You use it to meet the universal basic need of autonomy and being able to express yourself as a human being. When you do this, you recharge your body and mind, top up willpower stores, and put yourself in a better position to handle the stressors of life.

This me-time is already built into our society. It takes the form of weekends and vacations. These are periods of time that we as a collective have deemed as necessary to charge our batteries and keep our quality of life high. However, in our fast-paced society, along with financial issues for some people, these recharge times end up getting squeezed to the point where they feel non-existent.

While many people might get weekends off from their job, many times their responsibilities as a parent are just beginning. Sports, activities, and other obligations can easily eat away at your me-time. This can cause all sorts of unwanted side effects, from emotional eating to depression.

For a lot of people, they put everyone else first at the expense of themselves. When things get busy, the first thing/person to get cut is themselves.

That needs to change. Part of this healing process is learning how to get yourself back on the priority list. We could argue all day about whether you should be priority number one (you should be, by the way), but regardless, you should at least be ON the priority list.

Taking care of yourself and your needs means you are better able to not just handle life, but to thrive in it. That means you are at your best for others and for yourself. No one suffers when you are taking care of yourself.

I recommend that you have this me-time every single day. For some people, this might seem like an impossible task. It might require you to have a discussion with your partner and work together as a team.

Deanna and I make sure we have our own time each and every day to do whatever it is we want. We also split up the weekends to ensure that we each have a day free of responsibilities and can just be a human being for once. Saturdays are her days and I take care of the kids. And Sundays are my days when she takes care of them. Although I can't say that without also saying that there are plenty of Saturdays when she helps me out. Point being, communication is key, but we know that these days are available to us and can look forward to them to recharge.

While you don't have to do what we do, you absolutely should be finding time for you, and often. When you don't, negative side effects occur. You start feeling like a shell of a person. Recovery is impacted. And you're not managing your fatigue optimally. If you're not careful, this can create a downward spiral or keep you stuck in a state of stasis where very little personal growth and progress happens.

So get yourself on the priority list. Communicate with whoever you need to in order to get any help you need. Whether you work a 9-5 or are a stay-at-home mom/dad, you still deserve to have your basic human needs met. And it will only improve the lives of everyone around you.

PART IV:

RELATIONSHIP WITH MIND

CHAPTER 14

IDENTITY CHANGE

The Identity Tree

Transformation comes not from changing what you do, but by changing who you are. And changing who you are is about building a new identity.

Everything you do and have in your life is a function of who you are being. Every action you take and outcome you experience is a side effect of the identity you've created for yourself.

On our journey, we get so focused on what we want and what we have to do to get it. But actions and results are just outcomes. They are a side effect of who we are being.

I like to illustrate this concept with what I call an identity tree. Picture a tree with roots going into the ground, a trunk rising from the ground, and then branches and leaves coming from that trunk.

Now, when it comes to our life, the roots are our identity, the trunk is our behaviors, and the branches and leaves are our outcomes. So our outcomes naturally flow from our behaviors, which are born from our identity.

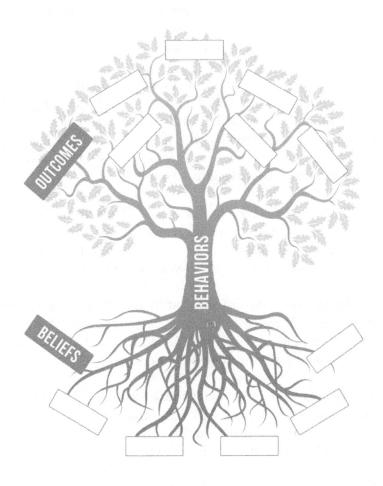

Our identity is made up of our thoughts, beliefs, and values. It's the framework from which we live and experience our life. These beliefs can be limiting or they can be empowering. They are the operating system that drives the actions we take.

Most of us focus on what we want in our life. You want to lose 20 pounds. You want to wear a bikini. You want to look fit. These are all outcomes. We don't do outcomes. They happen. They are side effects of our behaviors, aka results.

A smaller percentage of us focus on what we need to do – the strategy. This is OK; it's a step in the right direction, and of course, our behaviors matter. But they aren't the be-all-end-all and shouldn't be where you focus most of your attention.

You can focus on the trunk and the branches all you want, but unless your root system is taken care of, your personal growth is going to stall. Your beliefs influence your behaviors, which influence your outcomes. So if you want to change your outcomes, you can't just water your leaves – you have to get down to your roots and address your beliefs.

The beliefs you have around food will determine what food means to you. And as we discussed earlier, the meaning you attach to food influences how you interact with it, which will affect how much you eat, what you eat, and why you eat.

The beliefs you have around your body will determine how you treat yourself, and whether your behaviors will come from a place of self-hate and rejection, or self-love and acceptance. And this will determine the health of your body.

The beliefs you have around exercise will determine what movement means to you. This will influence the type of exercise you do, how much of it you do, and every other decision you make with it. And that, of course, will affect your outcomes.

Your behaviors naturally flow from your belief system. And your outcomes naturally flow from your behaviors. If you want to implement healthy behaviors, they must be layered upon an operating system (your beliefs) that is in alignment with your desired outcomes.

If this sounds kind of out there to you, and you're someone like me who needs more science and practicality, then you only need to look at the placebo effect to feel more grounded. The placebo effect is rooted in the idea that our thoughts, perspectives, and beliefs influence our outcomes. It's so powerful, in fact, that scientists have to design studies to account for its influence.

So yes, set some outcome goals. Let them be your north star. Attend to your behaviors. Ensure they will lead to the outcomes you want. But be sure you take the time to understand and change your underlying beliefs, as that's the level where true transformation happens.

Limiting Beliefs

When we don't stop to question our beliefs, we end up taking them as truths.

False truths are dangerous. Beliefs are not always facts. When we assume they are, we end up being blinded to helpful information that could improve our lives. We filter out all evidence that runs contrary to our beliefs, and we only see the information that reinforces our current belief system.

This cycle can work for you or against you. Empowering beliefs create an upward spiral of improved life experiences, reinforcing those beliefs.

Limiting beliefs create a downward spiral of diminished life experiences reinforcing those beliefs. In other words... you feel stuck.

This is important to understand because you can choose to subscribe to whatever beliefs you want, and whether they are universal truths or not doesn't matter. All that matters is that they are your truth. And whatever truths you choose to live by will determine the outcomes in your life you achieve.

Empowering beliefs and perspectives will lead to more favorable outcomes than limiting beliefs and perspectives. So when you aren't living the life experience you want, you need to look beneath the hood and see what beliefs you're choosing to subscribe to, and decide which ones need to be challenged and cut.

We have a lot of limiting beliefs surrounding our goals. We tell ourselves stories that we've accepted as truth, when in reality, they are just beliefs we've taken from experiences that we've made part of our identity. Then we live this identity. We act it out. And we get the results of it.

The experiences we have are determined by the beliefs and perspectives that our life situations are layered upon. These beliefs and perspectives create our identity. This is the reason why if you want to change your life experience, you need to change your identity. From that identity flows behaviors that are in alignment with it. And those behaviors will lead to a series of outcomes.

Your beliefs and perspectives are the reason why two people can watch the same house burn down, yet experience the situation in very different ways. If one of those people was living three states over watching it happen on the evening news, their experience will be different than the actual homeowner watching their house burn down in person. The house burning down (the situation) is the same, but the way each person is perceiving it is different. This will lead to a different life experience.

That might seem obvious, but we can take that same example and look at it another way. Let's say we have two different people who are each watching their own homes burn down. Again, this is a very similar situation for each person. Yet if one person believes the fire destroyed everything that meant anything to them, while the other person sees the situation as an opportunity for a fresh start, they are going to have very different life experiences. Each person brought a different identity into the same situation. These identities were made up of different beliefs and perspectives, which lead to different results and experiences.

IDENTITY CHANGE

Your identity interacts constantly with your environment. The beliefs you have about your body will determine how you eat and how you exercise. It will determine your confidence and your self-worth. It will influence how you interact with the world and whether you take certain chances with your career or relationships. It will impact your entire life experience.

The beliefs you have about food or exercise will dictate how you interact with them. Limiting beliefs will force you to see these things as body manipulation tools. You might always feel like food has power over you or that exercise feels like a chore. This will keep you stuck in Diet Culture behaviors, which will negatively impact your life experience.

Here's the thing – we aren't aware of most of our limiting beliefs. They are so rooted in our identity and so accepted as fact that we've never stopped to question them. But once you realize that beliefs are why you are where you are today, you suddenly start becoming hyperaware of your thoughts and actions and why they happen. You stop trying to force external behaviors and outcomes and start trying to influence them naturally by internally changing your identity, beliefs, and values.

This is the reason why we've spent so much time in this book changing the way you think about food, body, exercise, and mind. We're cultivating a new identity. Tips and tricks and other neat little strategies that Diet Culture promotes and that people are drawn to only lead to you developing limiting beliefs and negative experiences. It's the reason why so many people feel stuck and frustrated living through the same cycle for decades.

But when you become aware of and challenge your beliefs and perspectives around food, body, exercise, and mind, you open yourself up to creating a new, more empowering identity. And this identity will then interact with your environment in a more productive way. You see food differently. You see your body differently. Exercise takes on a new meaning. And all these beliefs coalesce into a life experience you can be happy with.

Self-Sabotage

Most people already know what behaviors are good for them. We don't need more doctors and nutritionists telling us to eat more vegetables. We don't need people telling us that we should be exercising. What we need is more people explaining to us why we struggle to do the things we know we should be doing to live the life we want.

That's where self-sabotage enters the picture. How many times have you tried your best to incorporate healthy behaviors into your life only to talk yourself out of them eventually? The mind is extremely powerful. It can rationalize any behavior it wants.

It's the reason why I truly believe more people need a therapist than they need a nutritionist. Everything we do and achieve starts with our psychology. That's why this entire book is based on healing your relationships with food, body, exercise, and mind. These relationships exist in your mind, and your behaviors naturally flow from the meaning you've attached to each of them.

You create a problem when you focus too much on behaviors, actions, and strategies and ignore creating an empowering identity. You create cognitive dissonance. In other words, how you are acting is in conflict with who you are. Your behaviors don't align with your beliefs. Something feels off. And what typically happens in that scenario is you're able to engage in these behaviors, but only in the short term. You white-knuckle and willpower your way through the process. But you can't act out of alignment with who you are for an extended period of time. When your behaviors are in conflict with your identity, they don't last, and neither do your results.

This is one of the biggest causes of all self-sabotage. It's the reason you know what you need to do yet you don't do it consistently for life. It's the reason you keep starting and stopping healthy behaviors, give up on your workouts, or feel like you aren't worthy to be loved and accepted as you are right now. It's rarely the lack of desire that holds us back. It's that we don't believe we possess the power to change our lives to the degree we want.

Remember the Identity Tree? The roots (your beliefs) of the tree manifest the trunk (your behaviors), which then creates the leaves and branches (your outcomes and results).

Too many people are trying to insert a behavior into an belief system that doesn't align with it. It's like trying to install a new program into an operating system that has faulty code. When you try to act in a way that is out of alignment with your beliefs, this new behavior has no solid ground to support it. It exists through willpower alone.

So you're only able to maintain it as long as willpower isn't depleted. Once depleted, whether from a demanding day or from something else that requires it, the temporary behavioral supports disappear, and you're left with the core foundation – your beliefs, aka your identity.

Trying to build a habit on top of a misaligned belief is like trying to build a house on top of water. The behavior has nothing to latch on to, and when that happens, your current beliefs swallow up your best of intentions. You rationalize skipping your workout. You talk yourself into eating things you know won't make you feel great.

Essentially, you revert back to the identity you were before, because you never really changed it. So your behaviors once again become aligned with who you are and always have been.

To stop self-sabotage you have to align your behaviors with your beliefs. That means first becoming the person you want to be by challenging all the limiting beliefs that are keeping you stuck as your old identity.

These limiting beliefs are keeping you tethered to a past version of yourself. They are your current operating system. And they will continue running your old program and giving you the same behaviors and results until you change them.

Imagine yourself at your Ideal Body. Remember, your ideal body is the body you're in when you have healthy relationships with food, body, exercise, and mind. It's when you're no longer obsessing about food, when you feel comfortable and confident in your own skin, and when you're living your full life experience. Who is this version of yourself? How do you feel? Don't focus on what you have or what you look like at your Ideal Body. Focus on who you are and what you believe about yourself and how you choose to show up in your life.

Your goal is to step into that future identity – today. To act in alignment with the person you want to be. Notice the differences in your current and future identities and start questioning your current beliefs that don't align with your desired future self. Where did these limiting beliefs come from? Are they always true? How are they holding you back? What new empowering beliefs can you replace them with? What beliefs do you want to bring into your future? You have a choice. You can change your beliefs. And in doing so, you can change your identity and your life.

Once your identity changes, you approach your journey differently. Instead of asking yourself "what do I do?", you start asking yourself "who am I?". You focus less on the things you need to do and more on the person you need to be. And with the latter, you automatically know what to do. You get to a point where you don't just believe you can do it – you know that you will. It's a done deal. It's who you are.

You're someone who takes care of themselves and respects their body? The choices you make will be in alignment with that identity. You don't talk yourself out of them. It's who you are.

Self-sabotage doesn't enter the picture because you're behaving in accordance with your beliefs.

Change Your Past

So much of our past influences our life to this day. We had experiences that created an imprint in our minds. These emotional bookmarks are then held for us and are used to interpret the events of the now.

For example, if someone called you fat when you were 15 years old, and that moment created feelings of shame and embarrassment, then an emotional bookmark was created. And this bookmark holds its place via the use of a belief.

Going forward in your life, this belief is used to filter your world. It influences the way you think, feel, and act.

Being called fat at 15 creates a belief that being a certain size is shameful and that other people will judge you and make fun of you. So going forward, you act in a way that will avoid that pain.

These emotional bookmarks and beliefs are constantly being created through experiences. The more traumatic, the stronger the emotional bookmark, and the more deeply rooted the underlying belief becomes.

Understanding this, you might think that the past is the past and there's nothing you can do about it. The past can't be changed, after all. Or can it be?

The past only exists in our minds. The original experience is over. It's the beliefs that live on to the present moment.

These beliefs are what make you relive that past experience over and over again. It's like you're stuck in a loop. The original experience created the belief, and now the belief is forcing you to relive that original experience. The longer it goes on like this, the more reinforced it becomes.

Why does this matter? Because your past and present are experienced through the lens of your current beliefs. That's what your life is – a never-ending series of experiences that are shaped by your beliefs.

So you can change your past (and future) by creating new beliefs. No, you can't go back and change the original event, but you can change your past in all the ways that it impacts your present and future.

That's what matters most anyways. You don't have to carry the trauma of your past anymore. You can choose to let it go. You can choose to change your current beliefs so that you experience your past differently. Because how we interpret our past has less to do with our past, and more to do with our present.

Being called fat at 15 doesn't have to impact your life at 40. Being rejected at 25 doesn't have to influence your self-worth at 50. Nor does being criticized yesterday have to change anything about who you are or how you act today.

Remove the emotional bookmark of your past by changing your beliefs of the present. And let your future unfold using your new empowering beliefs of today.

CHAPTER 15

MOTIVATION

Instant Transformation

On one random spring Wednesday, I received a call from my Dad asking me to come and help him. My mom had fallen down, and she was having a hard time getting back up. My dad wasn't able to help her up by himself.

I didn't think too much of it at the time. He had given the phone to my Mom, and I talked to her to see what had happened. Apparently, she had fallen down the day before when she was coming back in from getting the mail.

She sounded really tired and exhausted, and seemed to be in physical pain. I immediately left the house and drove 15 minutes to go help out. But when I got there, it was a completely different scene than I had imagined.

My mom seemed kind of out of it. She was talking to me, mumbling, and her thoughts didn't make much sense. I scooped her up and laid her in the bed that was right next to where she was laying.

As I talked to her, her speech was getting more and more slurred. And it almost seemed as if she was about to fall asleep right there

205

and then. It was at that time I realized what really was going on – she had had a stroke the day before when she fell.

We called 911, and an ambulance took her to the hospital. It was confirmed. She had a stroke. A piece of cholesterol had broken off and blocked several parts of her brain.

Interestingly enough, I came to visit her in her room later that day once she was settled in recovery. We were talking. Her speech was a little slurred, but nothing too crazy. However, the whole left side of her body could barely move.

We both laughed about the situation as we tried to cope, but spirits were still high, as she was going to be starting rehab, and most people improve at least a little through the process.

But that's not what happened. Over the next 3 months, my Mom never left the hospital. She stopped eating. She lost all functionality on her left side. And slowly but surely, she lost who she was as a person. Then, she passed away.

I was devastated. I was extremely close to my mom. She came over every Wednesday night to watch my then 8yo son so that Deanna and I could have a date night. And she watched him for an entire weekend every month so we could have a kidless weekend. That doesn't even include the weeklong vacations we'd take a couple times a year.

She was a fully independent person... until one unexpected day, she wasn't.

I tell you this for two reasons – one, tell the people you love that you love them. Life is short, and you never know when you won't get the chance to do it again. And two – this experience completely changed my life.

Her death was a wakeup call for me. Over the next year, I gave up a 20+ year near daily marijuana habit, learned a foreign language, learned the piano, started meditating daily, picked up running, biking, and swimming, stopped binge eating, and wrote this book, among other things.

These were all things I always wanted to do but either I tried them and didn't stick with them, or they just remained a desire or wish in my life to accomplish before I died.

This experience taught me that I didn't want to live a life of regrets. I didn't want to be in the hospital wishing I had done all the things I wanted. I had a moment of instant transformation – an inflection point in my life that changed the trajectory of it forever going forward.

This kind of thing happens all the time with people when they go through a traumatic experience. Someone has a heart attack, and they quit smoking, start working out, and get healthy. Someone loses a loved one, and they have a wake up call that they could be next.

But you don't have to experience the trauma that I did to feel motivated to achieve the things in your life you've always wanted. All you need to do is gain perspective on life and what's important, and then live as the identity you want to be in the future – today.

I became someone overnight. My behaviors hadn't even changed yet, and the new outcomes certainly hadn't manifested yet. But as I've said many times, behaviors and outcomes are just lagging indicators of your identity. And your identity can be changed in an instant.

This is the kind of motivation you want. It's pure. It's you. And it makes it easy to act in alignment.

On the rare occasion I feel a desire to slack off on my healthy behaviors, I channel the strength of my Mom, which is essentially the new life perspective I created from the experience I had with her.

You need to figure out why you're doing this. You need to go deeper than surface-level weight loss. Generate a new experience right now by getting in touch with your purpose and how you want to live your life without regrets. And then start being that person today.

Be Pulled

Too many people are trying to implement a healthy lifestyle while fighting unnecessary internal resistance. They take a behavior-centric approach that is rooted in surface-level habit change philosophy, which creates a dependency on willpower for taking action.

When this scenario is present, everything you do feels like a grind. You're always searching for motivation and inspiration because your willpower tank is always running on empty.

We think of motivation as this force that pushes us to our goals. But that's not the kind of force we want. That kind of motivation makes our journey feel like an obligation and all our behaviors feel like mandatory errands we need to take care of.

This kind of motivation requires an over-reliance on willpower and discipline to get you through the day. And make no mistake, that's what it feels like – a daily grind to just make it to the next day, the next week, or the next month.

No one can live like that. No one can sustain that kind of energy long enough to fully realize their true potential.

The motivation we want doesn't push us to our goals. It pulls us towards them. You're no longer pushing the snowball up the mountain. You've reached the peak and the momentum pulls you down the other side.

This kind of motivation is born from identity and healing your relationships with food, body, exercise, and mind. When these underlying relationships are healed and you're at your Ideal Body, healthy behaviors come to you.

When you have an unhealthy relationship with exercise, it's really hard to implement a daily workout habit. Yet that's what everyone tries to do. When you think of exercise as a tool to manipulate your body and self-worth, or you don't enjoy it, or you only do it for a future outcome, it's extremely difficult to push yourself to exercise.

You end up relying on willpower and little tips and tricks to get you to work out. You lay out your clothes the night before to make it "easier" to work out. You talk yourself through taking things one little step at a time. And you put all kinds of accountability strategies and rewards in place to ensure you take action.

Look… if that's what you have to do to get yourself to work out each day, you're going to struggle. If laying out your clothes the night before is the thing that makes or breaks your decision to work out the next day, you have bigger problems to solve.

Don't get me wrong, these tips and tricks can be useful, but only when they are layered upon a healthy relationship with exercise. And only if they are used to get you over the occasional hump of resistance. When the occasional hump is a permanent fixture in your life, there are underlying issues with your relationship with exercise that need your attention.

This goes for all 4 relationships – food, body, exercise, and mind. The surface level tips and tricks are only effective when layered upon a healed relationship. Otherwise, you end up relying on willpower to get you meal to meal, pound to pound, workout to workout, or happy moment to happy moment.

That kind of motivation is fleeting. It comes and goes and requires constant renewal.

But the motivation that is naturally born from you being healed and at your Ideal Body is a force that attracts your desired behaviors like a magnet. The force is always present, always pulling aligned outcomes to its source of attraction – you.

Once you realize what you really want is a full life experience, that will be the moment that momentum shifts and you see the light at the end of the tunnel. You won't feel this overwhelming motivational force. Instead, you'll feel a sense of peace, calm, and acceptance. Motivation will now feel like a habit that happens on autopilot. You've finally figured it out. And a new exciting journey is just beginning.

If You Were the Only Person In the World

What is currently motivating you? What is making you get up in the morning and take action towards your goals? Are you being driven by internal desires? Or are you being forced into action because of external pressures?

There's a question I like to ask myself and my clients to help them determine the kind of motivation that's part of their journey. It's a sort of filter that shines a light on whether the actions you take will be enjoyable, sustainable, and thus – effective.

The question is – "If you were the only person in the world, would you still want to _____?"

MOTIVATION

The blank could be anything. For many people, it's "lose weight." But it goes for everything – what you eat, what you choose for exercise, how you view your body, etc.

What this question does is it removes one of the biggest external variables from your motivation – other people. It gets you thinking about whether you're taking action for you because you want to, or for other people because you feel like you have to. It helps separate your internal desires from external pressures.

If being the only person in the world means you would no longer want to lose weight, what does that mean? It means you're currently being driven mostly by pressures to change your external appearance in order to conform to societal beauty standards.

Is that bad? Not necessarily. It's not so black and white. We do live in a society, as opposed to a deserted island, so there will always be some pressure to conform. But when that conforming is your everything, that's when bad things start to happen.

You start living for the future. You hate the process that is supposedly going to get you to your desired outcome. You focus on aspects of your journey that actually take you further from your goals. And your consistency and adherence suffer because every behavior you engage in is only contingent on what it will do to your body.

That's what the question helps you figure out. It allows you to take a quick glimpse into the future to determine whether what you do now is actually going to work out in the end.

The same goes for the exercise you choose to do or the food you choose to eat. If you were the only person in the world, would you still do the exercise you do? Would you do any at all? What about the food you eat? Would what you eat change? Why or why not?

The question shows you whether you're exercising for enjoyment and experience, or for body manipulation. It shows you whether you're using food as a tool to change the way you look, or whether it's a resource to feel your best. It shows you what matters to you.

Vanity goals are extremely motivating for people, especially at the beginning of a weight loss journey. But they are extremely hard to maintain. It takes a long time for visual changes to appear – usually longer than you can sustain the willpower to keep taking action. And that's what you're relying on when you don't enjoy the process. So willpower runs out before you get the future payoff of body change that you are expecting. When that happens, you get to the place most people find themselves in and you start to question whether all your hard work is worth it. You start asking, "What's the point?"

If that's the question you're going to end up asking yourself, you might as well ask yourself it now – before you even get going. What is the point? Why are you doing this? Would you be doing this if you were the only person in this world? Why or why not? What will keep you taking action regardless of what you look like or weigh?

For me, my motivation is now born out of the desire to live my full life experience. I got fed up with devoting so much time, thought, and energy to molding my body into something that would appeal to others so that I could feel better about myself. I got tired of obsessing about calories and my next meal before I had even finished the one I was on. I hated the body insecurity I lived with that kept me from pools, beaches, and friends.

I just wanted to live my life to the fullest. I wanted to be able to physically use my body in a way that gave me amazing experiences in life. And I wanted to stop letting my perception of my body hold me back from putting my authentic self out into the world without fear of judgment and rejection. I was tired of playing small. I knew my life could be so much bigger. And ever since I found my real "why", not only has my fitness changed, but so has my business, my social life, and every single thing my self-image had held me back from accomplishing all my life.

Take action for you because you want to instead of feeling like you have to. Take action because your "why" feels like a purpose instead of pressure. Purpose is infinite energy and potential. When you find your purpose, aka your "why", there will always be wind at your back and momentum pulling you forward. This kind of motivation doesn't expire. It is a part of you.

Setting a Thrive Floor

You're not always going to have sky-high motivation. That initial spark and drive you typically have when starting on a new goal is going to wear off. When that happens, you're going to have to find other ways to stay motivated. And as I discussed earlier, the purest source of sustainable motivation comes from cultivating an identity whose focus is on purpose and healing.

But even with an optimized identity, there are still going to be ebbs and flows in your drive, attention, and intention. You're not always going to feel like devoting the same amount of emotional energy and time to your health and fitness goals.

This is normal. It happens with everything we pursue, whether it be goals, hobbies, or general interests. We have seasons of life that can last months or even years. And we have other parts of our life that we'd like to move up the priority list, either by choice or by need.

The key to navigating these seasons is to have what I call a "thrive floor". This is the minimum amount of time, effort, and emotional energy that you personally need devoted to your specific goal in order to not just survive – but to thrive at it.

Obviously, this thrive floor is higher than zero effort. Unfortunately, zero is where most people in Diet Culture end up reverting to, and it happens shortly after that initial spark wears off – well before they ever cultivate an identity that will sustain and motivate them for life.

Your thrive floor is also obviously lower than your thrive ceiling – the maximum time and energy you are able to devote to any one goal at a time. Your goal is to stay fluctuating between your thrive floor and your thrive ceiling for the rest of your life.

You'll likely be at your thrive ceiling when you're first starting out on your Ideal Body journey. This can last quite a while – months or even years. But there will come a time when it isn't so high up your priority list. Maybe work is getting really busy, or the kids need more of your attention lately. These things get bumped up your priority list, and your Ideal Body journey gets pushed down a little. It might go from number 1 down to number 3 or 5, but it doesn't drop off your list altogether. It stays high enough on your priority list that you still thrive as an individual.

So you're going to have to look at your journey and identify the key components that are driving the majority of your success – the 20% of thoughts and behaviors that are resulting in 80% of your desired outcomes.

Your daily focus habits are sure to be part of that 20%. And they very well could be enough for you to thrive during those lull periods. And when the spark to devote more of your time and energy to your Ideal Body journey arises again, which it certainly will, you have a solid thrive floor to build on. You're not starting over from zero – trying to erase the last few months or years worth of neglect.

My thrive floor might be higher than yours, as I help other people do this for a living and prefer to have a higher floor than others. But to give you an example of what my life looks like during these periods, I always maintain my daily focus habits.

These include my daily morning walk, my morning smoothie, and listening to personal development every single day (usually on my walk). In addition to these habits, I also write about health and fitness at least once per week. And in our Elite community, I show up every Monday to set my weekly intentions, and I show up every Friday to find and share my breakthroughs.

This is my bare minimum in order to still thrive. I hit this thrive floor maybe once or twice a year for a few weeks. Sometimes it's for a few months. The year my mom passed away, it was longer than usual. When things get busier at home with the kids for only a week or so, it's shorter than normal.

So your goal is to know your own thrive floor so that you always stay engaged and moving forward with this journey. Because everything we do has ebbs and flows. And if you keep the ebbs above your thrive floor, then you can make huge leaps during the flows.

You Do What You Value Most

In any given moment, you're doing what you value most. That doesn't mean the behavior you're engaging in is a good one. Nor does it mean that particular behavior is what you want to be doing, or that it was even an enjoyable experience. It just means you're doing what's most important to you.

This can be a hard concept to understand, as many people will look at their life and assume they'd rather be doing other things – healthier things, more enjoyable things, or anything but what they're currently doing.

But desiring to do something else doesn't override your built-in value system. You will always gravitate towards what you value most in any particular moment.

You could have the best of intentions and desires to get up an hour earlier to work out. But if, when your alarm goes off, you hit the snooze button and roll back over, there's something you value more than working out – sleep. When you choose not to work out, it's not because you don't see value in doing it, it's because in the moment you saw more value in the thing you did instead.

You might desire to be on a vacation on the beach right now. You might think that has more value to you. But unless you're on the beach right now, you are currently valuing something else more.

Maybe you're valuing your bank account or maybe you're valuing the comfort you're feeling from not having to ask your employer for time off. Whatever it is, you're valuing something else more than the thing you desire to be doing.

This is important to understand, as many people struggle with motivation. They want to improve their health and fitness and start implementing some new behaviors, but they really struggle to get and keep them going.

For a new behavior to be incorporated into your life, it means something else must be replaced. All 24 hours of your day are currently filled. Your hours might be filled with sleep, eating, work, TV, rest, phone scrolling, reading, staring into space, or anything else. But every last second is occupied.

Most importantly, every last second is filled with what you value most in that moment. So to replace a behavior, you have to understand what it is you're valuing in that moment so that you can find other ways to meet that need.

Willpower can only override this value system in the short term. It's a sort of value suppression tool. But unless the value in the new behavior outweighs the value of the old behavior before willpower runs out, you will revert back to the old behavior.

MOTIVATION

So what do you do? When you want to implement a new behavior, identify the behavior it's going to replace, and the need it's meeting that you are currently valuing. Then, find other ways of meeting that need.

Sometimes this just requires shuffling your day around. For example, working out later in the day if you value sleep more.

Other times it will require you to, in essence, devalue the undesirable behavior you're trying to replace by changing your perspective and limiting beliefs.

For example, if you want something from someone but are afraid to ask because you don't want to be rejected, then devaluing your need to feel comfortable, by overcoming your limiting beliefs, can help you take the action you want.

Moral of the story – if you want to be doing something different with your time, you're going to have to dethrone whatever is currently occupying that space. And for any new behavior to be implemented, it is going to have to hold more value to you than whatever it's replacing.

CHAPTER 16

TRANSFORMATION MINDSET

Struggles & Breakthroughs

A member of our Built Daily community submitted a great question for our weekly live coaching call. She had been triggered by her body and was listening to our Fitness & Sushi podcast. On the episode, Deanna and I were sharing our own personal struggles.

When this member heard us talking about our struggles, she thought, "If these professionals, in charge of teaching me how to feel better about myself, can't feel ok about themselves, then why am I bothering?"

To be perfectly honest, when I first read it, I felt a bit of shame. She's right… who am I to teach people how to get over their food and body struggles when I struggle myself? I spent the day thinking about this question and reminded myself of one very important fact – to struggle is to be human.

As a society, we have this utopian view that we aren't supposed to struggle. We see happy people, confident people, people who seem to have their shit together, and assume they don't struggle. They do.

Not a single person will honestly tell you they don't struggle. In fact, it's the struggle that leads to the breakthrough of a better life. The discomfort of the struggle is the currency of transformation.

It's not about never struggling. It's about learning to navigate the struggles more effectively and growing. It's about normalizing them so you stop trying to avoid them, and instead, embrace them as opportunities for personal growth.

Nobody wants to struggle. It's uncomfortable. I like my comfort zone as much as the next person. It feels good. But here's the thing – change doesn't happen in your comfort zone. And let's be real, it can be very uncomfortable in your comfort zone anyways. There's discomfort in hiding from your struggles and spending a lifetime dieting and hating your body. And there's discomfort in facing your struggles and growing. But only one of those discomforts is going to result in an improved life experience. So if I'm going to choose to be uncomfortable, I'm at least going to expect a positive outcome to come along with it.

Struggles lead to breakthroughs. Your breakthroughs are born from your struggles. They are opposite sides of the same coin. For every struggle you overcome, you experience a breakthrough that will change your life. The bigger the struggle, the bigger the breakthrough.

That is what transformation looks like. It isn't pretty. It doesn't look like what you see in transformation photos. It's not an external phenomenon – it's an internal remodeling of your mind, of which your physical body becomes a side effect.

Transformation isn't some distant outcome of the future – it's an ongoing process that happens in the now. It's that moment that you don't give up. Each and every time you struggle and break through, you experience transformation. You transform yourself over and over again – for a lifetime. Each breakthrough changes you on a deeper level. You think differently. You see yourself differently. You act differently. And that's when new outcomes are created.

The before & after photos you see aren't transformation – that's just body change. There are plenty of people who experience transformation without any change in external appearance. That's because transformation is a change of identity. You change who you are. You take on your struggles and become a different person. And as a result, your life experience changes and improves.

The more you can understand this, the more you can stop running away from the discomfort of struggle. Because avoiding it isn't going to fix anything. It will only push the same struggle into the future to be dealt with at that time. Struggles never disappear unless they are directly addressed.

You've been so close to changing your life so many times already. You've taken dozens of different approaches, and they've all led you to that inflection point. This convergence to a single moment happens for a reason – it's a test to see if you're ready for the other half of your journey.

Future you, the one who lives a life feeling free around their food and body, is looking back at you just waiting to meet you on the other side of that inflection point. It reminds me of a metaphor of a dog wearing a shock collar for an invisible fence. They stay within their comfort zone of the backyard because the boundary of it is painful. But there is no physical barrier holding you or them back. There will be pain to overcome if you want to break free, but your freedom is on the other side. It's time for you to break through that invisible fence and live the life you've always wanted.

This pain and discomfort are assets in disguise. They are guideposts letting you know you're on the right track. They show you exactly what's standing between you and transformation. The wall of struggle is there to show you where you need to go – not where you need to stop. In time, you will even welcome them – seeking them out because you know a breakthrough is on the other side.

Everyone who has ever achieved something great in their life has experienced struggle. And the greater the achievement, the greater the struggles. The most successful people have struggled and failed the most. They just know how to use struggle as a means to empowerment, instead of letting struggles keep them stuck.

Deep down, we know this is true. Yet we still try to take the easy route. We take pills. We follow cookie-cutter meal plans. We think we're going to discover some kind of shortcut. We think we're going to change without experiencing transformation. But when you avoid the struggle, you're avoiding transformation. The only way to get to the outcome you want is to go straight through it all. No detours. No shortcuts.

If you can change your mindset and start seeing struggle as a good thing, in time, you will start to trust the process. You will experience the cause and effect of seeking out and persisting through the struggles. You will experience the breakthroughs and change. Each time this happens, you will grow more confident in your ability to overcome obstacles, and more excited about the personal growth that's imminent.

Setting Intentions

Every Monday in our Elite community, we set our intentions for the week. Everyone takes a few minutes to write down and share what they plan to focus on.

Intentions are very similar to goals, but there is a slight nuance to them. For starters, goals have a certain meaning attached to them that make them pass/fail. We are even taught that SMART goals (specific, measurable, attainable, realistic, and time-bound) are the best way to approach your desired future.

I disagree, and in practice, we've found that these goals fail at attainment just as much as diets do. Why? Because they are outcome-focused and very black and white in nature. You either achieve them or you don't. You either succeed or fail.

That reinforces the idea that transformation is some specific event in the future, as opposed to an ongoing process of struggles and breakthroughs. A SMART goal is something like, "I'm going to lose 10 pounds in the next month." Yes, it's specific, measurable, attainable, realistic, and time-bound. It checks off all the boxes. Yet I'm sure your experience has shown you that this goal usually doesn't get achieved.

Intentions are different. Intentions are like putting on a new pair of glasses and seeing your world through a new lens. If your intention is to work on your emotional eating struggle, then you end up navigating your environment differently. You see food differently. You notice different emotions. You become more aware of your unmet needs. And you don't beat yourself up when you don't fix a lifetime struggle in one week.

Your intentions are like goals, but they don't have to be fulfilled and crossed off your list for them to be effective. Intentions allow you to see your world differently and gather information and data that you wouldn't otherwise see. As you internalize this input, it interacts with you on the identity level, and you tend to gravitate towards your desired experience over time.

Goals aren't bad. They are nice to have as a sort of north star. They allow you to have a general idea of the direction you're going. But beyond that, most people don't achieve the goals they set for themselves and maintain what they achieved. SMART goals plus willpower can get you results; it's called dieting. You can lose 2lbs this week or 10 pounds this month, but if you're just focused on the outcome at all costs, results will be temporary.

Intentions are process-focused. They help you tune into what you want to work on. They redirect your attention to what matters and allow you to filter out all the environmental inputs that don't.

Will you "achieve" your intention the week you set it? Maybe, but maybe not. Either way, it is not a failure, because intentions aren't pass/fail. Most of the time, you will set an intention and then will continue to set that same intention week after week. Each week you continue making progress. You address your struggles and have small breakthroughs. You're never starting over.

There are times when I'll work on trying to improve my weekend eating for an entire month. Each time I "wave" through the weekend, I gather more information. My intentions allow me to see my weekends differently. I'm more self-aware when they come, and the intention lenses I'm wearing allow me to see the inner workings of my relationship with food better.

I make it through the weekend and I assess and think, "I wasn't really needing that particular food. I already felt satisfied. Next week, if it feels right, I will try eating this other thing instead." Then when the weekend comes and the action fits – I plug it in. I might go through this process for weeks or even months.

But that's the difference between intentions and goals. Intentions allow you to actually heal and improve your relationships with food, body, exercise, and mind. Struggles finally get overcome. So results are then permanent. Goals just attempt to get you to skip to the end outcome by a circled date on the calendar. The struggles just get bandaged over. Everything you do becomes a means to an end. And the results, if they even happen, rarely last.

Process vs. Outcome

Diet Culture has a tendency to make us too outcome-focused. Everything we do then becomes a means to an end. We try to strong-arm our calorie intake. We try to force the number on the scale to go down. And that usually ends with you feeling frustrated, or worse, wanting to give up.

The frustrations you feel on your Ideal Body journey tend to be a sign that you're being too outcome-focused. Anyone who has ever asked, "What's the point?" when the scale isn't moving the way they want it to has experienced this frustration.

Picture a spectrum. On the left, you have the Process. And on the right, you have the Outcome. When things get unbalanced and you start getting too far to the outcome side of the spectrum, you're going to be frustrated, and your motivation is going to be at risk.

The reason is simple – outcomes aren't in your direct control. And any time you try to control something that isn't in your control, frustrations will start to mount.

Outcomes can be influenced, but only when you are directly engaged with the process of the now. Outcomes are things that happen. They are side effects. They aren't things you do, so you have to stop treating them as behaviors.

Losing weight is not a behavior. Eating xxxx amount of calories isn't a behavior.

These are both outcomes. They aren't things you do – they are things that happen. They happen when you stay engaged with the process of healing your relationships with food, body, exercise, and mind.

The process is the journey. It is the now. And it is the only thing in your direct control. It's also the thing that makes up 100% of your life.

TRANSFORMATION MINDSET

The outcome is in the future. But the future only exists in your mind. So sacrificing your now for a future that isn't real or guaranteed is a great way to feel miserable every step of the way of your Ideal Body journey.

The path to your desired destination is through your journey. Your journey is life. It is all you have. It is the process. And it is in your direct control.

When you become too outcome-focused, all you see is where you aren't. Time slows down and your journey feels like a daily grind. You get caught up in sacrificing your days for a lower number on the scale in the morning. And when the number isn't what you hoped for, yesterday was a loss. You lose time. You lose life. You feel frustrated. And you want to throw in the towel even though you know your behaviors are good for you.

Being too outcome-focused means you're focused too much on the destination. You eat for weight loss in the future instead of eating to feel your best right now. You exercise to burn calories in order to move the scale down in the future instead of moving your body because you enjoy it and it feels good right now. You become extra focused on what your body looks like, how much fat is on it, and all its imperfections, instead of acknowledging all that it is capable of right now.

But it's not about being all outcome or all process-focused. Remember, it's a process vs. outcome spectrum, which means there's a middle ground that balances your needs of the moment with your desires of the future.

Your goal is to ensure you recognize when you've drifted too far to the outcome side, and then make the adjustments to bring yourself back more towards the middle. Because that's where sustainable motivation lies. That's where you'll find purpose, peace in your body, freedom in your eating, and joy in your movement. It's where you'll find improved consistency and adherence, and more effortless action. It's also where time becomes more of a friend than an enemy. Because the fastest way to experience your outcome, both in perception and in reality, is to be more present. And presence is found in the process.

So if you want to stay motivated, you need to find the intrinsic value in the now, also known as the journey. Eat because it makes you feel good – now. Move your body because it's enjoyable – now. Look in the mirror and appreciate what your body can do for you – now. That's how you stay consistent long enough for your desired outcomes to manifest.

Dealing With Mess-Ups

You are going to mess up eventually. You're going to eat something you didn't mean to. You're going to miss a workout too. These mess-ups are to be expected. It's what you do after they occur that matters most.

The key is for you to get right back on track with your next healthy behavior. That might mean getting back to productive thoughts, or it might mean getting back to productive actions. You're never off plan if you expect mess-ups to happen and get right back to the behaviors you want in your life. It's part of the process. And if it's part of the process, you're right on track.

This might seem obvious, but getting right back to the thoughts and actions you want in your life is not what most people do. Instead, they overcompensate for their mess-up. And that's the real problem.

Habits are formed through repetition. Without repetition, they never get a chance to seep their way down into your subconscious so they can happen on autopilot.

So when you accidentally overeat, what do you do? Most people think in averages. They assume that if they overate by 500 calories, all they have to do is undereat by 500 calories the next day and it's no harm no foul.

Technically this is correct. But weight loss isn't a technical struggle – it's a behavioral/psychological one. What you do and think long-term will have a bigger impact on your results than average calories. Besides... averaging two unwanted behaviors does not turn them into a good one.

Remember how I said habits are formed through repetition? Well, what do you think is going to happen when you get a whole bunch of overeating repetitions in followed by compensatory undereating behaviors? That's right – you're going to become a very good over and undereater. You're also going to habitualize all the destructive thoughts that come with those behaviors, like guilt, frustration, and fear of weight gain.

If your goal is to achieve your Ideal Body, then you need a good relationship with food, body, exercise, and mind. You get there by getting in reps with the thoughts and behaviors that will lead to those improved relationships.

So when you mess up and overeat, you don't overcompensate – you get right back to the behaviors you want in your life. You build the habits you want instead of unknowingly making destructive behaviors part of your normal life.

Your success towards any goal, whether that be health, weight loss, strength, or endurance, is more correlated to consistency than it is to the number of calories you eat, the types of food you eat, or how much exercise you do. Living your life on a rollercoaster trying to average everything is not practicing consistency, and it's not going to change you. It'll keep you right where you are and will make you more of what already isn't working.

Think of a horizontal healthy habit line. This is where all your wanted thoughts and actions reside. Your job is to spend as much time at this line as you possibly can. If you veer from this line and overeat, you should immediately return right back to this line. This is where you feel your best, and the longer you can spend feeling your best, the better your life will be.

If, like most people, you overcompensate, you shoot right through the line and end up way under it. You spend no time at it and get no repetitions in at your healthy habit line when you do that.

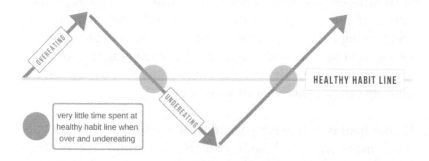

So if you mess-up, go right back to the line. This won't be your natural inclination though. That's normal. It's the old you trying to control an outcome. But the new you's job is to stay engaged with the process. So you'll have to retrain your thinking patterns to do that. If you mess-up, go right back to the line.

Lift the Deadlines

Weight loss deadlines force you to work against the clock instead of with your body. Yet we've all looked at a future date, whether it be summer, a vacation, or a wedding, and have attempted to calculate how many pounds we'd have to lose each week in order to be at our goal in time.

In the short term, this can work. Physique competitors do it all the time. And you might have even experienced a period of consistent weight loss in your past. But in each of those scenarios, the progress was unlikely to last beyond that deadline, if you even made it that far.

Why? Because your weight loss pace is not determined by how big of a deficit you're in. This is an overly simplistic way of looking at things. This is paper weight loss and only stands up in a technical world. In the real world, your pace is determined by the number of struggles you have and the degree to which you need to overcome them. The bigger the struggle, the more time it will take to overcome it, and the longer it will take for weight loss, if it's going to happen, to be reflected.

Sure, you can play the 500-calorie deficit math game and aim for losing 1lb/week. But the only way you're going to maintain that progress for life is if the underlying pressures on your eating are addressed.

This is why I don't like placing deadlines on transformation. When you're up against the clock, you don't act in your body's best interest. You end up sacrificing your body's needs for your ego's wants.

Deadlines force you to place arbitrary ceilings on your calorie intake in an effort to maintain a particular weight loss pace – a pace that's usually much faster than what can be handled. So, hunger gets ignored. Cravings are dismissed. Energy plummets. Attitudes worsen. Performance decreases.
And if it seems like you're falling behind your self-imposed deadline, you double down on your efforts and dig yourself into an even deeper hole. You restrict calories more. You ramp up your physical activity. And you start feeling worse about your body and the possibility you won't reach your goal in time.

While you might begin to lose weight, your relationships with food, body, exercise, and mind actually get worse. And it's only a matter of time before these negative side effects are expressed on your physical body and you end up back to square one.

Instead, why not focus your attention on identifying and overcoming your struggles and let your Ideal Body take shape naturally at its own pace? Working through emotional eating issues, the binge/restrict cycle, rebuilding trust with food, body image struggles, limiting beliefs, and motivation problems are going to be much more productive uses of your time and energy.

This is the inside-out approach to achieving your Ideal Body. Transformation is the result. The outside-in approach, in contrast, ignores these struggles and focuses on calories in / calories out, eat less / move more, and the scale instead. Short term weight loss followed quickly by regain is the result. Remember, things like eating less and moving more and energy balance are of course important, but they are side effects of your relationships with food, body, exercise, and mind. Trying to manipulate them directly doesn't fix what's causing the problem in the first place.

Focusing on calories and weight loss doesn't make your real struggles go away. It just pushes them down the line for you to deal with at a later time. And by then, they've become more ingrained into your identity and are harder to overcome.

So let go of the future deadlines and focus on the struggles right in front of you. Masking those struggles with a deficit will never get you to your Ideal Body. The only way out is through.

CHAPTER 17

MENTAL DIET

Curate Your Environment

One of the first things I do when I'm trying to implement a new habit or hobby is to start to surround myself with the people, information, images, books, videos, and communities that contain the identity of who I want to become.

This is called immersion, and it's one of the most powerful tools on your Ideal Body journey. However, when used incorrectly, it will be one of the most detrimental influencers to achieving your goals.

So many of us are focused on our physical diet. We spend countless time and emotional energy trying to curate what we put into our mouths. We're constantly trying to bring in more whole foods and cut out the foods that don't make us feel our best. But then, when it comes to our mental diet, we don't give it much thought. Instead, the information we allow into our minds creates unnecessary resistance to the things we're trying to accomplish.

We touched on this in the Identity Change chapter. If you remember, our behaviors and outcomes are direct beneficiaries of our beliefs and identity. But what you might not realize is just how much our beliefs are formed from the information we consume, aka our mental diet.

Your mental diet consists of all the auditory and visual information you consume, both consciously and subconsciously. This includes, but is not limited to, social media, magazines, product marketing, TV, articles, and even the words of people – strangers and close relationships alike. Images and words you absorb have the power to either take you to your goals or prevent you from reaching them altogether.

When you have a good mental diet and intentionally feed your mind information that aligns with your desired identity, it provides a sort of lubrication for your behaviors. But when the information you consume is not in alignment with who you want to become, you create unnecessary resistance to new behaviors and habits. Everything feels hard. It feels as if you're dragging yourself across sandpaper. You face a strong headwind – requiring you to rely more on finite willpower to get you through your days.

The quality of your mental diet directly influences the quality of your behaviors and the quality of your life experience. I would even go so far as to say that your mental diet is more important than your physical diet, if only because your physical diet tends to be a side effect of the former.

Your mental diet affects whether you feel good or bad about your body. It can make you restrict calories or ignore your body's hunger cues when you shouldn't. It can make you live in fear of judgment. And it can even create states of anxiety that put pressures on you to cope using food.

Someone else's before and after weight loss photo celebrating a smaller body can trigger you to feel less-than. It can reinforce that your worth is in your body. And it can lead to you going on yet another diet that doesn't work.

Reading about eating 1,200 calories per day or cutting out carbs in order to lose weight from some credible person with a series of letters after their name can make you restrict food and calories when you shouldn't. It can lead to you ignoring your body's needs in favor of adhering to an arbitrary calorie budget, which just leads to inconsistency and disappointment in the end.

Hearing one of your friends talk about the diet she's on and how much weight she's lost, or listening to a friend talk about how much they hate their body, can influence the way you view your own. This can keep you from healing your relationship with your body and keep you stuck with a negative body image.

So, when you're ready to be someone different, aka transform yourself, you need to make sure your mind is immersed in the right environment. Trying to heal your relationships with food, body, exercise, and mind while you follow accounts on social media that are constantly showing before and after progress photos is not going to help you break your disempowering belief that your body is your worth. Constantly talking to your friends about diets and calories and how much you all hate your bodies isn't going to help you eat and see your body from a place of self-respect, self-care, and self-love.

Start feeding your mind with the same intention that you feed your body. Immerse yourself with people and information that align with who you want to be. Curate your environment in a way that pushes you to success. And cut out anything you're immersing yourself in that creates resistance to your goals.

Set Boundaries

One of the biggest contributors to your mental diet is the words and behaviors of the people closest to you. Our family, peers, friends, and co-workers all have their own belief systems that are constantly being projected outwards in many ways. And if you aren't careful, their thoughts can pollute your mental diet and throw you off track.

Very rarely do others do this on purpose. Most of the time, the people closest to you just want to share their own life and thoughts. Other times, they say things out of so-called concern for your well-being. But there are times when they will say things with the intent to hurt too. Whatever the case, it's going to be necessary for you to set boundaries so that you don't internalize information that goes counter to your goals.

I've experienced situations that needed boundaries many times. And so have all of my clients. From the clients whose spouses are always policing their food choices, to the critical parents who are always commenting on your body – there is no shortage of toxic information you're going to have to contend with.

You might have a friend who is constantly talking about her diet and weight. You might have a friend group that is always criticizing their bodies. You might have co-workers or family members who think it's best to always be questioning your goals under the guise of "trying to understand".

It doesn't matter what it is or the intentions behind it, anything in your environment that degrades your mental diet is going to add unnecessary resistance to your Ideal Body journey. And if you aren't careful, it can tempt you to the point that you go back to your past Diet Culture ways.

So what do you do? You set boundaries. And believe me, I know this isn't easy for most people. People don't like conflict. They struggle to stand up for themselves and say what they need. They don't want to rock the boat or create an uncomfortable situation.

But do you know what else isn't easy? Having your parents comment on your body every time you see them. Listening to your friend talk about how great her new diet is and how much weight she's lost, while you are trying to work through your emotional eating struggle. Having an arrogant or even abusive spouse shame or laugh at you because you ate a candy bar while you're working on healing your relationship with food. At least when you set a boundary, the discomfort has a future payoff.

You're going to have to ask yourself what the better approach is – setting a boundary, or working on not internalizing other people's beliefs and opinions. The latter is necessary regardless, but a boundary doesn't always need to be set.

If a situation happens infrequently, say you see a sibling during the holidays once a year and they're always talking about dieting, then it might not be worth the investment to establish a boundary. On the other hand, if someone is part of your day-to-day life, the emotional investment in a boundary is going to be worth the payoff.

Setting a boundary is simple. You respectfully say what you need and why you need it. And then you release yourself from any reactions.

Deanna once set a boundary with me. We were sitting down in our media room getting ready to watch some TV. She came in with some snack food. I made a comment teasing her about it, something like – "ohhh… look at what you have." To me, it was innocent. I had no ill intention with what I said. But for Deanna, it made her feel guilt and shame around food. It made her feel like her eating choices were being watched.

So what did she do? She simply said – "can you not comment on the food I eat?" And while I'm sure I got defensive, I honored the boundary she set. And the neat thing was that I could also count on her to not comment on the food I was eating. Like most boundaries, it is a win/win scenario even if it's hard for the person receiving the boundary to see past the initial defensiveness.

Stand up for yourself. Say what it is you need. Don't assume people know. And don't assume people will even understand once you explain why. They don't need to understand. They only need to honor what you're asking for in order to thrive as a person. If that person loves and respects you, then it shouldn't be an issue.

The Food and Body Police

As you work towards achieving your Ideal Body, you're going to come up against a few different kinds of food and body protagonists. These people can apply resistance or force to your thoughts and behaviors – neither of which are in your best interest.

Take the food police as an example. They are there to get you to stop eating the way you've decided, and they make you second guess the food choices that are best for you. On the flip side, you have food pushers. The food pushers try to get you to eat when you don't want to, and they too get you to make food choices that don't have your best interests at heart.

Food police and food pushers don't have to be separate people either. They can both be part of the same person, like one of your parents, or a friend that always has an opinion on how you should be eating. And here's the kicker – they can be someone else, or they can come from within your own head. That's right – you can be, and often are, both of these people.

Once you realize this, you're going to see food policing and pushing everywhere. You're going to notice the voice in your head telling you not to eat something because you won't be able to lose weight. You're going to hear it say, "just get the salad" when you're eating with your friend because you don't want to look like a pig eating what you really want. It's going to tell you to eat your Mom's lasagna even though you aren't hungry so that you won't hurt her feelings.

And then you're also going to hear the comments from friends and family. They'll tell you to "live a little" when you really just don't want to have donuts for breakfast. Or someone will be more blunt and shame you for ordering dessert to make sure you know that's a no-no if you're trying to lose weight.

And then you're going to have to deal with the body gatekeepers. These people will always be telling you that you should have a different body than the one you currently have.

Sometimes they'll say you need to lose weight. At times it'll be criticism. Other times it'll be out of concern for your health. Other people will tell you to stop losing weight. That you're getting too skinny. That you'd look better weighing a little more. And just like with the food police, the body gatekeeper could be you. You could always be telling yourself that you should look different. In the end, these people are simply projecting their own insecurities, beliefs, and desires onto you. Or if these people are you, you are just speaking your limiting beliefs into existence.

All of these things apply pressure to your ability to make choices that are best for you. Instead, you start making choices to appease other people. And you start creating feelings of guilt and shame which inevitably lead to inconsistency, frustration, and feeling stuck.

First things first – recognize and be aware of when it's happening, and whether it's originating externally from other people or internally from yourself. If it's coming from other people, then don't be afraid to stand up for yourself and defend your boundaries.

If you're not hungry, then say you aren't hungry. If someone is constantly commenting on what you eat and it's bothering you, then politely tell them you'd rather not talk about your eating choices. If the comments are about your body, then say you'd appreciate if they didn't comment on your body. You don't have to explain why, but you can if you think it'll help.

If the policing and pushing pressures are being applied from within your own head, then you need to recognize it, challenge the limiting belief, and then remind yourself to always make the choice that will meet your needs of the now, as that's what will make you feel your best in the long run.

Part of achieving your Ideal Body requires you to set boundaries in your life. It's a way of showing respect to yourself. It's not always an easy thing to do or talk about with people, but neither is living in a way that you don't feel your best.

Developing Your Mind

Your mental diet isn't just about curating your environment in a way that removes resistance to personal growth. It's also about consuming material that directly contributes to your personal development.

We want our identity to continually be evolving and transforming itself for the better. And the only way to do that is to feed your mind with information that allows for that growth.

Something I do is I commit to an hour each and every day to consuming some form of personal development content. Most days it's more than that, but at the very least, I listen to either a personal development podcast or audiobook on my daily morning walk. By the time 8am rolls around, I've already gotten in an hour of movement and an hour of healthy brain food. This calibrates my mind and body for a productive day. Each day, I grow and develop my identity just a little more, and then this new and improved identity interacts with my environment for the day.

10 years from now, I would be perfectly happy if my body didn't change. In fact, I'd be thrilled if I maintained my Ideal Body for the next decade and it was as healthy as ever. However, if in 10 years I'm still the same person and haven't grown, then something went wrong. The goal is to continually be understanding yourself and life better and to be able to live your life to the fullest of experiences. And you can't do that if you aren't developing your mind along with your physical body.

Reading, watching, and listening to content, or even putting yourself into positions to have new experiences, all feed your mind with new input that drive your growth. This growth changes your identity, which influences your behaviors, which affects your outcomes in life.

And here's the really neat thing – all personal growth has carryover to other parts of your life. Improving your health and fitness transfers over to your relationships and other aspects of your life. Developing your spirituality impacts your health and fitness. Learning about personal finance can change the lens through which you view the rest of your world.

In fact, most of the breakthroughs I have with health and fitness nowadays come from the things I learn from other passions, such as business, finance, or even my hobbies. Because when you consume this content from the point of view of a particular identity, you filter the information through that identity. And that helps you to fill in the holes and make connections that enable you to have breakthroughs.

When you develop your mind along with your body, you create a synergy and an upward spiral – allowing one to feed on the other. Your diet and movement create a physically healthy brain structure that is able to assimilate information that helps you grow. And then this information influences your diet and movement behaviors for the better.

This is the reason why keeping your mind stuck in Diet Culture is inhibiting your growth and preventing you from experiencing transformation. It takes more than eating chicken breast and fruit to transform yourself. Losing weight doesn't change who you are either. You have to change your identity. And to do that, you have to intentionally and consistently feed your mind information that allows you to grow.

CHAPTER 18

INTENTIONAL CALIBRATION

Are You Ready?

As you work your way through the healing process, there might be some specific goals you'd like to pursue. Even though you might've achieved some improved fitness, health, and weight loss by overcoming your struggles, you might want even more of these things, or even something else. This is where intentional calibration comes into play.

During the healing process up until this point, you were still calibrating – it just wasn't intentional. The changes that happened to your body, health, etc., were just natural side effects of you healing your relationships with food, body, exercise, and mind.

Intentional calibration comes AFTER you've achieved a version of your Ideal Body. Let's call this your Ideal Body version 1.0. It is the body you have once you've healed your relationships with food, body, exercise, and mind.

Notice how intentional calibration is the last chapter of this book. That's because it should come last – after you heal. Diet

THE IDEAL BODY FORMULA

Culture does this backwards. It starts with an extreme form of calibration and doesn't even get to the healing part.

It's important not to start intentional calibration until after you've healed, for a couple of different reasons. First, healing is what will drive the majority of your progress. Too many people are eager to get through the healing so they can start calibrating. But healing will net you 80% of your results. If you're still struggling with things like emotional eating or motivation with exercise, then healing and overcoming these struggles will have a much bigger impact on your health, body, and life experience. So don't try to skip to the end. Stay focused on what matters most.

And the second reason to wait to implement intentional calibration is because during this process you're going to have to be self-aware enough to recognize when adjustments you're making are taking you out of alignment with the Ideal Body Formula. If you haven't healed yet, then you won't know what a healthy relationship with food, body, etc., feels like. So it'll be hard to know when you've taken things too far and things are getting dysfunctional again. If you're not there yet, that's OK – healing is still calibration, and will still result in fitness, health, and body changes.

At version 1.0 of your Ideal Body, these relationships might not be perfect, but you've improved them enough to understand them, and you're well on your way to being happy, confident, and living a fuller life experience. So feel free to experiment with intentional calibration at this point.

Notice how I've been talking about version 1.0 of your Ideal Body. This is because your Ideal Body isn't static. It will continue to change and evolve as you do. Remember, your Ideal Body is a side effect. That means any changes to your behaviors or mindset have the potential to create changes to your body.

INTENTIONAL CALIBRATION

If you suddenly find a love for running and start training for a marathon, you're very likely to burn more calories, and that is going to influence your energy balance and your body. This new change in behavior might take you from Ideal Body Version 1.0 to Version 2.0.

Or maybe you discover a new fondness for smoothies or salads, and this ends up displacing some other more calorically dense foods in your diet. You weren't necessarily trying to eat fewer calories. However, that was the result of you trying new foods and wanting to continue eating them. This then influences your energy balance and potentially changes your body. Now we're on to Ideal Body Version 3.0.

Over your lifetime, you are going to potentially have hundreds or even thousands of versions of your Ideal Body – each one simply being the side effect of new thoughts and behaviors that remain in alignment with the Ideal Body Formula.

Understanding how this process naturally works, we can use it to pursue our individual goals in a healthy and productive way. This is what we call Intentional Calibration.

While weight loss could potentially be a goal for you, it is far from the only goal you might have. I've worked with clients who wanted to use calibration to improve their health, to build muscle, to work on specific exercise goals, or to even gain weight. The point is that there are any number of goals you might want to pursue, and calibration is the process you'll use to ensure you're approaching them and progressing in a way that always keeps you at your Ideal Body.

So if you want to lose weight because your joints are hurting or because it'll make you a faster runner, you can. If you want to build some muscle because it makes you feel empowered, you can. If you want to improve your health because you want to live a long life, you can. Or if you just want to have a certain look, you can. You have the autonomy to direct your life without feeling guilted or shamed for having these goals.

But what you need to understand is that there are limits to how far you can take these goals before you take yourself out of alignment with the Ideal Body Formula. And once that happens, your relationships with food, body, exercise, and mind start to become dysfunctional again, and your life experience begins to suffer again as a result.

So it's going to be essential that you know when to push and when to pull back, how to go about making the changes to your behaviors, and when it's time to accept that you've done all that you can reasonably do.

Making Adjustments

Your goal in the calibration process is to make small changes to your eating, exercise, and mindset – all while staying in alignment with the Ideal Body Formula. That means you make a small adjustment to your eating, gather feedback, and assess whether your relationships with food, body, exercise, and mind remain in a healthy place.

This is in contrast to Diet Culture's process, which focuses on the outcome and tries to white-knuckle changes to your diet and exercise. Its process starts with the question, "How much weight do you want to lose: 1 pound or 2 pounds per week?" If it's the former, then you cut 500 calories from your diet, set a calorie budget, and you hold the line. If it's the latter, you cut 1,000 calories and double down on willpower to maintain that arbitrary calorie intake.

With the Ideal Body Formula, if you want to make an adjustment to your eating, you look for places that it makes sense. For example, maybe you want to lose weight, which would require you to eat less than you are now – all else being equal.

INTENTIONAL CALIBRATION

Your number one priority isn't to eat less. It's to stay in alignment with the Formula. That means, first and foremost, any changes you make need to ensure that your diet remains satiating, satisfying, and nourishing. You shouldn't feel restricted or deprived, and your eating shouldn't become a means to an end. The goal is for you to feel your best, without obsessing over calories or your eating as a whole.

Yes, you might need to eat less, but eating less doesn't have to mean restriction. Restriction is a feeling – a mindset, not an action.

You can eat less without feeling restricted. You can also eat less and feel even more satiation, satisfaction, and abundance surrounding your food. That's the goal. In fact, that's the only way you're going to succeed with body transformation goals for the long term.

When I was looking to lose some weight, I first assessed my diet as a whole. Were there any places I felt like I was maybe a little too overfull? Was there any meal that would be easier to adjust than others?

In my case, I was feeling a little too full at night, yet I really enjoyed having a little something that was satisfying while I watched TV. Normally, I was having some Greek yogurt with granola and frozen blueberries. But while I loved the meal, I was still kind of full from dinner a couple of hours before.

I also had another problem – I really liked my nighttime meal and didn't want to give it up. So I looked at my other meals and asked myself if any of them could be swapped for the Greek yogurt. My afternoon meal of chicken, beans, corn, rice, and cheese was probably my least favorite meal. When my goal is to eat less, I start cutting out foods that I DON'T enjoy as much. That seems like such an obvious thing to do, yet most people do the opposite – assuming that if they like a particular food a lot that it must not be good for losing weight. But it's so much easier to let go of the foods you don't enjoy than it is to sacrifice all the ones you do. So I swapped that meal out for my Greek yogurt meal, and at night, I decided to have a cookies and cream frozen Greek yogurt bar instead.

This had a very interesting effect. My afternoon chicken meal had been around 500 calories, but it wasn't very satiating. I was always really hungry when it came dinner time. Ironically, when I swapped it out for my 300-calorie Greek yogurt/granola/blueberry meal, I ended up more satiated and more satisfied on fewer calories. And when nighttime came, I felt a perfect level of hunger to have my cookies and cream Greek yogurt bar, which by the way, was 200 calories less than the meal I used to have.

So what happened here? By prioritizing my body's needs, I was able to eat 400 calories less each day while also improving my satiation and satisfaction. Not only did this fulfill my goal of losing weight, but it improved my consistency and it was easier to adhere to.

This is why it's so important to not prioritize calories and eating less at the expense of your body's needs. When that happens you end up honoring your weight loss over your needs, and consistency and adherence will always suffer in the end.

Now, had I made that adjustment and my satiation, satisfaction, or nourishment had decreased to levels that lead to feelings of restriction, deprivation, or more inconsistent eating, then I would have simply gone back to how I was eating before. You assess the data, ask yourself if you're in alignment, and then determine whether to continue with the new plan or go back to the old and try something else.

Never do you veer from the Formula, which means never are you not at a version of your Ideal Body. Your Ideal Body joins you every step of the way through the calibration process. In contrast, Diet Culture has you making arbitrary, outside-in slashes to your calorie intake to try and take you from a body you're ashamed of, to a body that conforms to societal norms. But in the end, you just end up ashamed, undervalued, inconsistent, and a continued victim of Diet Culture.

100 Calories = 10 Pounds

Diet Culture teaches us to cut 500-1000 calories from your diet, depending on whether you want to lose 1 or 2 pounds per week (who ever chooses just 1 pound, by the way?), engage in some kind of workout that melts the fat off your body, implement a no-excuses mentality by doubling down on willpower and discipline, and all your struggles from the past 20 years will be wiped out in a few months. Right?

Wrong. Look... I'd love if that were the case. And sometimes the math seems to justify that thinking on paper (2 pounds per week times 10 weeks equals 20 pounds, or 2 pounds a week for a year is over 100 pounds). But rarely does that ever play out in the real world while also maintaining those results for the rest of your life. Yes, there will always be an example of someone doing it, but remember not to confuse the possible with the probable.

Remember, weight loss isn't the same as transformation. Transformation is about change of identity. That is permanent. The pursuit of weight loss directly via the arbitrary restriction of calories is not transformation – it's body change. Many people will say they don't care and that they'd be happy with just the body change, but body change is fleeting when it isn't the byproduct of transformation.

Your goal during the calibration process, whether your desire is to lose weight, gain weight, build muscle, get stronger, get healthier, build endurance, or any other goal, is to approach it with the understanding that small changes done consistently over long periods of time are what lead to the outcomes you want.

Most of the negative consequences we've experienced with our health have been the byproduct of years of accumulated thoughts and behaviors. Most adults have gained weight gradually over the years. It only takes a 100 calorie daily surplus to gain 10 pounds in a year. Over 5 years that's 50 pounds. In reality, a 30lb weight gain over 30 years is the result of just a 10 calorie surplus per day. That's it.

Of course, you probably didn't experience weight gain so linearly. Most likely there were periods of ups and downs that coincided with the diet cycle you've been stuck in for a lifetime. Lose 10 lbs over a couple of months. Gain 12 back over the following one. Rinse and repeat for 30 years. Or experience a sudden gain of weight over a few months to a year due to a life situation, and then never really recover from it.

The point is this – if you want to reverse this process, you have to start thinking differently. You have to get away from Diet Culture's idea of express delivery of outcomes and instead look at goal seeking as a long-term calibration process built upon an underlying foundational principle of consistency.

It doesn't take huge, sudden changes to reverse the trend of weight gain or suboptimal health. It just takes small changes, done consistently from this point going forward – forever.

Just a 100 calorie daily deficit accumulated over a year is the equivalent of 10 pounds. Change a few small things in your eating and movement and you have the potential to lose a lot of weight without feeling like you're dieting.

Fix the 1400 extra calories you eat every weekend because you feel restricted, deprived, or the need to cope with your emotions using food. There's 20 pounds right there.

Burn an extra 200 calories a day because you start doing exercise you enjoy and get consistent with it. There's another 20 pounds.

This is what healing your relationships with food, body, exercise, and mind accomplishes. Its goal is to get you consistently making the best choices for yourself again. In doing so, small changes to energy balance, movement, food choices, emotional coping strategies, body image, etc., incrementally add up over time and change you.

So understand that a daily smoothie for the next 20 years will have more of an impact on your health than a perfect 2lb/week weight loss diet done for 3 months followed by 6 months of "regular" eating. Understand that a 100-calorie deficit, created naturally because you've neutralized your emotional eating by directly addressing your needs, will have more of an impact on your weight than a 10-week "fat loss diet blitz cleanse no-excuse challenge."

Get consistent by healing your relationships with food, body, exercise, and mind, and then remain consistent while you calibrate and make small but sustainable changes. Then set it and forget it. Changes are happening in the background while you live your life.

Utilizing Tools

You started off your Ideal Body journey by ditching the scale and giving up calorie counting. This was necessary in order for you to heal your relationships with food, body, exercise, and mind.

When you're first starting on this new journey, you are very susceptible to the influence of past Diet Culture thoughts, beliefs, and behaviors. These tools keep you anchored to that past life and prevent you from turning inwards and getting in touch with your body.

But as I talked about in the earlier chapters, the scale and calorie counting are just tools. They are neither good nor bad. Using them successfully is completely dependent on the person using them, their state of mind, and where they are in their journey.

Since we are now in the calibration chapter, that means you've already ditched these tools, healed your relationships, and are at a version of your Ideal Body. This is the time to consider reintroducing these tools.

However, based on the experiences of the countless people who have been through our program, once you've learned to live and thrive without them, it's possible you won't want to use them again. You start the program having a hard time letting them go and finish the program not wanting to have anything to do with them.

But that doesn't mean you can't use them. There is a certain subset of individuals who use the scale and calorie counting to some degree and thrive using them. I am an example of one of those people. Deanna, on the other hand, cannot use them without them dragging her back into food and body obsession.

When it comes to our clients, I've found that about half of them end up using at least one of those tools. But more often than not, it is not a daily use kind of thing, but a targeted tool when the situation calls for it.

Consider calorie counting, for example. There are different levels of counting: from calorie awareness to quantifying, to targeting – all the way to calorie budgeting. And I'll break these down in the next section.

You might decide to experiment with calorie counting in some way at some point. When used right, this process will be less about suppressing how much you eat and more about understanding your food better. Maybe you just want to understand how much you're eating relative to your hunger signals. Or maybe you need a little more information about your food so that you can make a more educated adjustment.

Whichever level you use, you don't have to take any of them to the extreme. In other words, there's a difference between adding up the calories of a single meal because you're curious, versus tracking every last morsel of food that goes into your mouth every day for the rest of your life.

My preferred personal use of calorie counting is using it when I want to change up my core meals. If I know my current core meal at lunch is 500 calories (because I quantified it), then I can create and try out a new meal based on that nutrition level. If weight loss is a goal, I can try to find a 400 calorie meal. If weight and muscle gain is a goal, I can try to find a 600-700 calorie meal. Whatever the case, the meal must at least equal, but preferably improve my levels of satiation, satisfaction, and nourishment. And rule number one is: if any use of calorie counting pulls me back into Diet Culture and food and body obsession, I kick it to the curb – immediately.

What about the scale? How can that be used in a way that keeps you in alignment with the Ideal Body Formula? Similar to calorie counting, it can be used at different frequencies (daily, twice a week, once per week, etc.) or at different times in your life (that random week in the summer vs. the 2 weeks during the holidays) to help you understand yourself and your behaviors better.

Weighing yourself shouldn't result in an emotional drive to change your behaviors. That's what used to happen to you before you healed. A number on the scale would trigger you to compensate by changing your eating. You'd end up using outcome-based behaviors in an attempt to control the scale, instead of addressing the dysfunctional relationships you had with food, body, exercise, and mind that were creating your struggle.

Instead, the scale should be a neutral data point – a tool that gives you an additional layer of information to help you achieve your specific goals. Remember, this might be weight loss, but it could also be weight maintenance or weight gain, depending on your health, performance, or even physique goals. The key is knowing when the tool goes from being an asset to a liability and being able to be honest with yourself so that you can give it up when it causes problems.

About half my clients will use the scale at some point over the period that we work together. And only about 20% will use it daily for that whole time. So as you can see, the scale isn't an all-or-nothing tool. It has a purpose depending on your goals at that time and where you are in your healing journey.

There are dozens of use cases for these two tools, all of which can be used successfully so long as you are already healed and at a version of your Ideal Body, and you're able to stay in alignment with those healed relationships during the calibration process. If you can't, then these tools should not be used. There are plenty of people who can use these tools in a healthy way and have them benefit their life. Similar to how tracking steps, sets, reps, and other aspects of your workouts can help you make informed decisions on your goals, calorie counting, and the scale can do the same when layered upon healthy relationships with food, body, exercise, and mind.

The Calorie Counting Hierarchy

Just because you haven't been counting calories up to this point doesn't mean you've been lacking awareness of your food. There's a huge space between being oblivious to what you're eating and thinking you need an honorary PhD in nutrition in order to eat well.

I like to think of calorie counting as a hierarchy. There are 4 different levels – each level building on the one below it. So, let's take a look at all 4 levels and the ones you need to be focusing on.

LEVEL 4	CALORIE BUDGETING
LEVEL 3	CALORIE TARGETING
LEVEL 2	CALORIE QUANTIFYING
LEVEL 1	CALORIE AWARENESS

The first level is called Calorie Awareness. During the healing process, this is where you spend all of your time. For many people, they will never go beyond this level. This is not a bad thing. The levels above this one aren't better in any way. In fact, for many, the higher levels are worse – triggering them and dragging them back into Diet Culture.

In level 1, you are simply aware of the energy density (calories) and the general nutritional makeup of your food. It requires a basic understanding of eating and a very basic education around food. This is all you will need to succeed with your eating. You don't need to spend hours or years studying nutrition to reach your goals. And for many people, they already have the education they need, as they've spent a lifetime educating themselves on nutrition and biology, thinking that was what was necessary to lose weight.

Level 1 means you know what kinds of foods are higher in calories and which foods tend to be lower. You know which foods tend to be higher in nutrients, and which foods tend to be lower. With this very basic knowledge, you can make the best choices for fulfilling the 3 variables of Intentional Eating – satiate, satisfy, and nourish.

This level means you know that peanut butter tends to be more calorically dense than an apple. It means you know broccoli is more nutritionally dense than rice. It means you know a chicken breast has more protein than oatmeal. And it means you know that cheese or nuts tend to be higher in fat than beans, or that pasta tends to have more carbs than cauliflower. None of these foods are better or worse for you. They all serve a purpose that can meet your individual needs. You will use this level 1 awareness to take you all the way through the healing process and achieve version 1 of your Ideal Body.

The second level of the hierarchy is called Calorie Quantifying, and it is where you'll start if you choose to utilize calorie counting as a tool during the intentional calibration process. This is the process of quantifying how much you're eating once you've already healed your relationship with food. You are essentially putting a calorie number onto how much you already eat naturally. Quantifying shouldn't influence your eating in any way. It is a completely independent process from your eating. Pretend like you're just eating naturally in a way that makes you feel your best, and someone, without your knowledge, was watching you eat and adding up how many calories you're eating. This is quantifying. It's an extra layer of information for your eating and can be used to understand your food a little better and to help you make more educated calibration decisions once you've healed.

The third level is called Calorie Targeting. Again, this is exclusively used for calibration after you've healed your relationship with food. And it's only used if you want to use it, or if you're able to, without it pulling you back into old Diet Culture thinking and behaviors.

Calorie Targeting is layered upon the previous two levels of Awareness and Quantifying to help you direct your eating to whatever goal you have. If quantifying your food intake showed you that you were eating 2000 calories, and you have a goal to gain weight, you can set a calorie target of 2300 calories as a way to create some directed intention behind your eating.

Calorie Targeting means that the target you set for yourself is a guideline or suggestion. It is not a line in the sand. If you set a goal to eat 1500 calories and nighttime comes and you are hungry – you eat. You always honor your body's needs without exception. If you go over your target, then you should feel neutral about it. If you feel guilty or feel the need to compensate, then you are not ready to use calorie targeting.

But again, you will ever only need the first level – calorie awareness, to succeed at achieving your Ideal Body. The other levels are reserved for calibration AFTER you've already healed. And used only if you can utilize them without falling back into Diet Culture. This is when specific goals come into play that could benefit from additional awareness tools. But they are never required.

The final level of the hierarchy is Calorie Budgeting. Interestingly enough, this is where 99% of dieters start, and it's the reason why they keep failing. You will likely never use this level – even after you've healed your relationships with food, body, exercise, and mind, and have achieved your Ideal Body.

This level is reserved for the .01% of the population. That's 1 in 10,000 people. These people tend to be fitness competitors or need their body to be in a specific condition by a specific date. This might mean an actor getting ready to play a role in a movie, a bodybuilder who is competing in 122 days, or a few select other situations.

Calorie Budgeting is not a permanent solution. It completely disassociates you from your body's needs and aims to force your body into a certain condition. The people I listed above know this, and they accept the resulting weight regain that comes as a consequence of calorie budgeting. A fitness competitor puts a lot of weight back on after a competition. An actor doesn't stay in movie shape permanently. They can't. Their body doesn't let them.

This level is reserved for a select few, yet nearly all dieters start there. They set a calorie budget of 1200 calories and try to hold that line at all costs. Hungry? Ignore or suppress it. Full? Eat anyways because you haven't hit your budget yet.

This process takes them further and further out of touch with their body's cues. And after a lifetime of doing this, they have no idea what hunger actually feels like or how they should be eating to meet their needs.

So remember… of the 4 levels of the calorie counting hierarchy, you will likely only ever utilize the first 3 levels. And of those 3 levels, you will only need the first level to succeed in healing your relationships with food, body, exercise, and mind, and achieve your Ideal Body. Levels 2 and 3 are there as tools for calibration if or when you want to use them, or are able to without slipping back into Diet Culture.

Letting Go of What You Can't Control

Too many of us worry about the things that are completely out of our control. When I was in my early twenties, I started losing some of my hair along the temples. When I first realized this, it was all I could think about.

I buried my face into the computer screen and researched all I could about hair loss and how to prevent it, or, even better, regrow it. I spent money I didn't have and wasted time on trying to solve a problem that was mostly out of my control, rather than doing more productive things.

INTENTIONAL CALIBRATION

I tied my identity to my hairline, and I was miserable as a result. My self-worth plummeted, my confidence dried up, and I thought my social life was over.

A good year later, after realizing the products I bought weren't doing a thing, I decided to give up on them. I stopped treating my hair in the morning, at night, and in the shower. I stopped checking my hairline for signs of hair regrowth every time I walked by the bathroom mirror.

And once I stopped doing that, I realized that I was the same person whether I had hair or not. It was me who chose to make myself miserable from that situation.

I eventually adopted the mantra: "do not worry about the things you can't control." And this mantra is just as relevant during your Ideal Body journey.

There might come a time on your journey when you've done all you can do to intentionally calibrate without falling back into food and body obsession and Diet Culture strategies. If or when that moment comes, you have one thing to work on – acceptance.

We've already talked about body acceptance. This is done during the healing process. It's about working towards accepting your body unconditionally as it is right now so that your behaviors come from a place of self-love and self-care. This makes it easier to eat and move your body in a way that is enjoyable and sustainable. Whereas hating and rejecting your body pushes you into outcome-based, punitive behaviors that are rooted in Diet Culture. These behaviors don't address your underlying struggles but instead attempt to slap a surface-level bandaid (dieting, cutting calories, burning calories, willpower, etc.) over your problems. And, as you've probably already experienced numerous times, these behaviors don't last, and they keep you stuck in the diet cycle.

THE IDEAL BODY FORMULA

Body acceptance isn't the type of acceptance I'm talking about here. If you're at a point where you're calibrating, you've already healed and embraced the body you're in. You might still have goals to change it, but you're okay with whatever outcomes happen during this process, as you're already at a version of your Ideal Body.

The type of acceptance we're talking about here is situational acceptance. This means being okay and at peace with your life, knowing you've made your best effort possible given your current unique circumstances.

This is not the same thing as giving up. It's the opposite, actually. It's about going all in – on you. You embrace yourself and all that you've accomplished. And learn to be OK with the outcome.

That doesn't mean you stop trying to improve and grow as a person. It just means, right now, in this moment, given your psychology, personality, circumstances, and genetics, you've pushed to the boundaries of what's reasonably possible for you. You understand that pushing yourself beyond this boundary carries negative consequences.

Because here's the thing – it's normal to want to weigh less, look or feel younger, be healthier, have more muscle, or be fitter. But it won't always be possible to push these goals as far as you desire without negative side effects showing up elsewhere. And you have to be OK with that. You have to be OK, knowing that you've done your best. And you have to respect yourself enough to know that pushing further creates more problems than it solves.

And that boundary is always changing. Maybe you're raising 4 small kids right now and you don't have as much time and energy to devote to your training goals. But in the future, when they are grown or out of the house, you might have more time and energy to devote to yourself. If you stay in alignment with the Ideal Body Formula, you will be able to take advantage of changes in your life circumstances. But only if you honor what is best for you in any given moment of your life.

Nothing is permanent, but the now doesn't change. So you have to learn to accept and embrace your situation of the now so that you're always living your best life possible for YOU – in any given moment.

CONCLUSION

JUST THE BEGINNING

From Mental Transformation to Reality

You've made it through the entire book! Hopefully, you feel inspired and confident to get started down a new path. You likely read a lot that resonated with you and changed the way you viewed your health and fitness journey. For some people, it's even going to feel like they've already experienced transformation. But I want to caution you.

Reading this book will not be enough to change your life. It's normal for people to read books and articles, watch videos, and listen to podcasts and other material, and feel like they made progress towards their goals. And in a way, you most certainly have. It's a start. Your identity is shifting. But there's more work to do.

Right now, you have what I call a mental transformation. This is when you consume information that leads to epiphanies, mental breakthroughs, and shifts in beliefs and perspectives. You've cultivated a new mindset. But if you stop here, your transformation will never become a reality. It will never manifest itself into your day-to-day life. It will never change your overall life experience in any meaningful way.

JUST THE BEGINNING

To make your transformation a reality, you have to take it from the abstract mental space in your mind to the physical reality you live in. And you do that by taking action. You do that by putting into practice all you've learned so that you can put yourself into a position of struggle, which, if you remember, is what leads to new experiences and breakthroughs.

There's a big difference between knowing and understanding something. You can read about riding a bike all you want. You can consume article after article about how to ride one. You can hire a coach that tells you how to do it. You could even teach others how to ride one based on the information you've read. But until you actually ride the bike, you will never KNOW how to ride one. You will only UNDERSTAND how to do it.

The knowing comes from doing. I can tell you how to overcome your emotional eating struggle over and over again. I can tell you to sit with the discomfort, identify your emotions and your underlying unmet needs, and find productive ways to cope. That process might be a revelation to you. It can even feel like you've fixed your emotional eating to some degree. But the understanding can also be a false sense of hope. The understanding can keep you stuck in the mental transformation space.

Until you actually take that process with you into an emotional eating episode and work through the struggle in real-time, the transformation will only ever exist in your mind. The experience is what allows you to collect data points that are unique to your situation. It's what allows you to apply what you understand. You learn about yourself. You become more self-aware. And you put yourself into positions that allow you to experience real transformation. A single real emotional eating episode experienced with the right mindset is worth 100 books. This goes for anything you are struggling with in regards to your relationships with food, body, exercise, and mind.

I'm emphasizing this because many people will finish this book and immediately start looking for more information to consume. They are very smart and intelligent people who know a lot about this stuff because they've learned a lot about it. They understand it.

Resist this temptation. Resist living in a horizontal transformation space. Take your transformation vertically. Take the next step up with action.

What will you change with your eating? What will you change about the exercise you do? Did you explore where the beliefs about your body came from? Did you take the Ideal Body Assessment (https://builtdaily.com/member-assessment/) so that you know where exactly you're struggling with your relationships?

If this book resonated with you in any way, you owe it to yourself to go deeper. Surround yourself with other like-minded people. Immerse yourself in the ideology. Get help when you need it. But be sure to act on the knowledge. You can't think your way to transformation. You need real experiences to really change yourself.

Commit to Never Dieting Again

The only way to succeed at your Ideal Body journey is to fully reject Diet Culture and everything it stands for. There is a temptation for people to want to straddle the fence between Diet Culture and the new Ideal Body. But this just keeps you in no-man's land.

I get it though. You understand why giving up calorie counting and the scale are important for the healing process. But you're tempted to sneak a peek at the scale, or you still add up calories in your head to give you a bit more comfort and control over your eating. This is completely normal behavior, but it's like trying to swim with an anchor tied to your ankle.

The Ideal Body Formula is the antidote to Diet Culture. They don't work in harmony. You can't take the antidote while sipping on the poison. So trying to take your favorite parts of both just leads to more failure and frustration. It's not going to work. For the antidote to be effective, you have to remove the poison from your world. You have to keep your distance from it. You have to commit to never dieting again. Don't dabble in the Ideal Body Formula – embrace it completely.

You already know Diet Culture doesn't work. Ten to fifty or more years of dieting and weight loss attempts are proof of that. You're reading this book because it didn't work. But I do understand. Diet culture is all most people know. It's a relationship they've had most of their life. They've shared emotional highs and lows together. They've been through a lot. So, like with any breakups, it can be hard to just sever the tie. Memories pop up of the "successes" you had together and you're tempted to give it another go. Just remember, this relationship with Diet Culture is toxic. Let it go and never look back.

I admit that can all sound a little dramatic. But it's for good reason. The pull to go back to Diet Culture is strong and it shouldn't be underestimated. You have to recognize when those thoughts and behaviors start to resurface so you can squash them before they take you over. I have witnessed plenty of people go back to Diet Culture tactics – cleanses, detoxes, 30-day weight loss challenges, caloric restriction, the next trendy diet. I see them still struggling years later, never breaking free. If you're not careful, this will be you too.

One year, 5 years, or even 10 years will pass you in a blink of an eye. You'll wake up and realize Diet Culture just consumed you that entire time and you never got anywhere. We've had people who joined our program who fell victim again to Diet Culture and went back to it, only to rejoin our program years later admitting that they just weren't ready to give up dieting yet.

That's why I'm being emphatic here. Ditch Diet Culture. Flat out reject it. Every single part of it. Get mad at it if you have to. Get fed up with its messaging that your body is your worth. Get annoyed when you see people promoting Diet Culture tactics, whether their intentions are good or bad. Stay surrounded by people who practice the Ideal Body Formula. And commit to never going back to Diet Culture no matter how tempting it might be.

Journey Expectations

I've gotten the opportunity to watch the Ideal Body journeys of thousands of people unfold. Not to mention, I can personally relate to their experiences because of my own transformation. And something I've noticed is there are very similar stages and patterns that people undergo on their journey. If you can understand this, you can manage your expectations and normalize the experiences you're bound to have.

For starters, the beginning period when you first decide to ditch Diet Culture and plug yourself into the Ideal Body Formula is a highly motivating time. Hope has resurfaced. You finally feel like there's a way out of your lifelong struggle. And make no mistake – this is the way out. However, this beginning period is also a very shaky stage. You are very susceptible to Diet Culture influences, self-doubt, and any struggles you encounter are real risks to you staying the course.

Understand that this is normal. You have a lifetime of programming to overcome. It takes time. During those first couple of months, it takes constant reinforcement, immersion, support, and a focus on curating your environment in a way that keeps you on track. That's why it's so important to make sure you don't do this alone and that you surround yourself with people who share the same philosophy as you do. Keeping any remnants of Diet Culture around you puts you at a heightened risk.

But if you can make it through that short window of time, you'll notice a shift in your thinking. You start to fully embrace this new life and you go all in on it. This is when the real transformation happens.

At that point, you are able to really see Diet Culture for what it is. The contrast between your new life and your old life gets stronger and stronger, and it gets easier to say no to Diet Culture. You start to see people who are stuck in Diet Culture differently and actually have compassion for them. This isn't you thinking you're better than them. This is you remembering how you felt and how much your life experience was negatively impacted when you had your worth tied to your body and you were constantly obsessing over your food and appearance and fitting into society's beauty standards. So in reality, you start having compassion for your old self, and you see your old self in others. This makes it so much easier to stay away from Diet Culture going forward.

That said, you aren't completely in the clear. There will be some temptations to go back to Diet Culture. You'll get triggered by your body. You'll have a bad body image day. Or a close friend or family member will have great "success" on a diet.

These experiences will challenge your beliefs. But resist the temptation to go back to a lifestyle that didn't work for you. These moments are what I call inflection points. And each one is an opportunity for transformation. They are opportunities to rewire your life going forward. So be sure to talk yourself through the situation using the strategies you learned in this book, and take the right fork in the road. Each time you do, you will make that path easier to take.

Every day, week, or year that goes by it gets easier to live your new life. Nowadays I'm so detached from Diet Culture that I don't even know what's going on in it. I hear about trendy diets long after they've reached mainstream. And I'm a health and fitness coach! My mental and physical environments are curated perfectly. I'm not around Diet Culture anymore. And when I am, I don't see it anymore, because my beliefs don't align with Diet Culture anymore, and my beliefs are the lens through which I experience the world.

So know that your Ideal Body journey is going to be similar. Manage those expectations so you know how to navigate the ups and downs. If the struggles are normalized, it makes them easier to overcome. At the beginning, just take things one day at a time. Stay surrounded by people who live the Ideal Body Formula. Create your support network during this sensitive stage. And if you can immerse yourself in this ideology for a couple of months, know that your new identity is forged, and your unique Ideal Body – the NEW Ideal Body, will be yours to experience.

What's Next?

It's time for you to start putting the Ideal Body Formula into practice and live it. And to help you do that, I'd like to invite you to join us in our Built Daily Mentorship program.

This is where we personally coach and mentor people through the Formula. Similar to this book, we walk you step-by-step through the process of healing your relationships with food, body, exercise, and mind, so that you can achieve the NEW Ideal Body.

But the big difference between the Mentorship and this book is the community, coaching, support, accountability, and the specific focus on taking action. A book can only do so much. You need to surround yourself with like-minded people. You need support and advice when you're struggling. And you need to know exactly what to do to implement the concepts I talked about in this book.

That's exactly what the Mentorship does. Deanna and I lay out a specific process for you to follow that leads to you naturally achieving your healthiest weight. We teach you the specific frameworks we've developed from over a decade of coaching clients that show you exactly how to implement the ideas in this book for your own unique situation. And then we personally coach you day-to-day through the entire process.

This isn't an informational program – it's a transformational one. It is focused on holding you accountable to taking action and getting you actual results. Because we are taking you by the hand and personally guiding and supporting you, we're able to get you to your goals in a fraction of the time it would take to do this on your own.

If this sounds interesting to you, your next step is to sign up for a free Breakthrough Call. On these calls, we'll chat about your struggles and your goals, and we'll put a strategy in place to get you to where you want to be. And if you want our help implementing that strategy, we can show you what that would look like too.

You can schedule your free Breakthrough Call right here – https://builtdaily.com/call/

You can also further connect with us by listening to our podcast – Fitness & Sushi. You can find it on Apple Podcasts, Spotify, or any of your favorite podcast players. On our podcast, Deanna and I dive deep into the topics of the Ideal Body Formula.

Finally, consider joining our email list. Deanna and I write every week and share our thoughts and Ideal Body strategies with the people in our community. We'd love to have you a part of that.

You can sign up for our free emails here - https://builtdaily.com/emails/

Remember… what you do next matters. Whether you join us in our Mentorship program or not, be sure to surround yourself with the people who share your desired thoughts, beliefs, perspectives, and goals. Commit to ditching Diet Culture forever. Take action on the Ideal Body Formula. And your Ideal Body will soon be a reality.